Praise for
The Wealth Chef

"Ann Wilson not only proves that nice girls can get rich, she does it in a way that's fun to read and easy to understand. A surefire recipe for living your life the way you want, free from concerns about money. In my book, that's rich."

Lois P. Frankel, Ph.D., author of
Nice Girls Don't Get the Corner Office, USA

"THE WEALTH CHEF is a must if you want to make your money work for you and become financially free. I wholeheartedly recommend it."

Katharine Dever, international speaker and business mentor, UK

"This is so much more than a 'financial self-help' book—it is an appetizer of food-for-thought, a main course feast of to-do list action plans and a cherry-on-top dessert of true empowerment and financial freedom, prepared by the best WEALTH CHEF of all—YOU!"

Nerina Visser, head of Beta Solutions and
ETFs at Nedbank Capital, South Africa

"I always dreamed that I might be a really rich grandma one day—but THE WEALTH CHEF has helped me realize that financial freedom can come a lot sooner than that—and taught me how to create a fabulous Wealth Feast now!"

Sofia Wren, author and healer, USA

"Thank you, Ann, for helping me learn to love money and get excited about creating wealth in my life! Since implementing The Wealth Chef Recipes, I've quite literally created miracles with my finances."

Michelle Clarke, business success coach, UK

"I wanted to work on my negativity, fear, and anger around money and get rid of my debt. THE WEALTH CHEF is inspiring, focused, honest and has, quite simply, set me on the road to success. To my surprise, I also had a lot of fun along the way!"

Susan Rodrigues, HR executive, Australia

"THE WEALTH CHEF gave me a great sense of relief, and helped me to realize that only now learning about money doesn't mean that I'm stupid, just that I was under-informed before, and has been a real life-changer for me."

Wendy Brooke, specialist horse trainer, USA

"Ann cooks up a storm in her financial kitchen, providing wealth recipes that will help you attain financial independence, and have fun getting there. Well-structured, practical advice and guidance about the route to financial freedom. THE WEALTH CHEF has every recipe you need to create your financial dreams."

Mike Brown, managing director of etfSA, South Africa

"Just one line saved my husband and myself $900 on our car insurance—and that doesn't even begin to cover all the other amazing stuff we've learned."

Nadhira Razack, founder of Comfy Sales, Australia

"Like a great cookbook, THE WEALTH CHEF gives you all the ingredients, tools, and recipes to control your money and create real wealth. Ann is an inspiration, and this book is how you will invite her into your life and let her help you become financially free too. You will be unbelievably glad you did."

Kate Emmerson, The Quick Shift Deva and author of *Clear Your Clutter*, South Africa

The
WEALTH
CHEF

The WEALTH CHEF

Recipes to Make Your Money Work Hard,
So You Don't Have To

Ann Wilson

HAY HOUSE LLC
Carlsbad, California • New York City
London • Sydney • New Delhi

Published in the United States by: Hay House LLC: www.hayhouse.com®
• *Published in Australia by:* Australia Publishing Pty Ltd: www.hayhouse
.com.au • *Published in the United Kingdom by:* Hay House UK Ltd: www
.hayhouse.co.uk • *Published in India by:* Hay House Publishers (India) Pvt
Ltd: www.hayhouse.co.in

Cover Design: Antigone Konstantinidou
Cover Image: 2/Bjorn Holland/Ocean/Corbis

The author of this book does not dispense medical advice or prescribe
the use of any technique as a form of treatment for physical, emotional, or
medical problems without the advice of a physician, either directly or indi-
rectly. The intent of the author is only to offer information of a general nature to help you in your quest for emotional and spiritual well-being. In the
event you use any of the information in this book for yourself, the author
and the publisher assume no responsibility for your actions.

Cataloging-in-Publication Data is on file at Library of Congress

Tradepaper ISBN: 978-1-4019-4666-1

1st edition, July 2014

Printed in the United States of America

This product uses responsibly sourced papers and/or recycled materials. For
more information, see www.hayhouse.com.

Dedication

This book is dedicated to my mom and my dad.

*Dad—thank you for planting the seed of possibility
in me, for teaching me that my financial well-being
is my responsibility and that as a woman,
I have everything I need within me to be, have,
create, and do anything I can imagine.*

Mom—thank you for teaching me how to love.

*The yin and yang of your gifts
have taught me true wealth.*

*Although neither of you are here to see
this book, I know you would be proud.*

Support the eradication
of poverty through women's
economic empowerment

All author royalties from this book are donated
to *The Small Enterprise Foundation.*

The Small Enterprise Foundation (SEF) is a
not-for-profit, pro-poor micro-finance institution
in South Africa. SEF works toward the eradication of
poverty by motivating women from the poorest households
to start or resume an income-generating enterprise,
providing them with a supportive environment where
credit and savings services foster sustainable income
generation, job creation, and social empowerment.

www.sef.co.za

Contents

1.

Welcome to the Ultimate Wealth Cookbook

Welcome! You're about to discover how to make your money work harder, so you don't have to.

Wealth and financial success are learned skills. You can learn to succeed at anything. If you want to be a great cook, you take a cooking course, you buy recipe books, you get to know your ingredients, and you practice. If you want to be a great golfer, you get a golf pro to teach you, you go to the driving range and practice your shots, and you get in the game to learn. And if you want to be wealthy, then, just like cooking or golf, you can learn how to do it.

It doesn't matter where you are right now or where you're starting from. What matters is that you're willing to learn. No one comes out of the womb a financial genius. Every wealthy person learned how to succeed at the money game—and so can you.

I also discovered that financial success is 80 percent about the person and only 20 percent about the technical skills. Eighty percent of the wealth that I've created in my life is a result of my mind-set.

The road to financial freedom is neither complicated nor difficult, though most people have been led to believe it is. The main reason so many people struggle financially is simply that they've never been taught the recipes for wealth.

I've had this book in my head for several years. I must have read hundreds of financial books and, generally speaking, I've found them to be very frustrating. They either gave me a great motivating story, telling me I needed to do something, but never exactly what; or else they were jam-packed with technical jargon that confused me and sent me into analysis paralysis instead of making me take action.

And some, to be honest, just bored me to tears.

The why, the who, the what, the when, and the how

The Wealth Chef is a step-by-step book that teaches you the why, the who, the what, the when, and the how! It provides anyone who has the desire to achieve financial freedom all the recipes needed to create abundant wealth, as well as the skills to master them easily and effortlessly.

Learning and mastering the recipes for wealth is about creating a gourmet banquet of your own life. It's about being able to feast on all the riches around us, sharing life's joys with those you love. It's about enabling you to get to the point where money is supporting you, not suppressing you, so that you can get on with the important business of living the big, shiny, purposeful life you came here to live!

Being wealthy is about creating, expanding, contributing, and leaving more than you took. It's about having the freedom to do what you want, where you want, and when you want to do it. It's about doing what you were meant to do.

If you want this in your life, read on! Here are the recipes you need to create the life you desire, as well as all the skills to ensure financial freedom.

Recipes and skills

Just like cooking, there are a series of fundamental basics that every person needs to master in order to have control of their finances, be able to weave magic with their money, and create a banquet out of their lives—a rich and tasty financial banquet. Few people, however, realize that, just like cooking, these basic money recipes are easy to learn!

At the very least, the five core Wealth Recipes will enable you to be a great Wealth Chef. You'll have all the skills, as well as the mind-set needed, to ensure you and those you love never go hungry, and you'll be on your way to financial freedom, where the money flows even when you aren't there to tend to it.

You'll be confident with your money management, you'll have control of your own financial well-being, and you'll understand how money works, how to bring it into your life, how to keep it there, and how to make it grow.

Once you've mastered the Wealth Chef basics, you may decide you want to create a bigger banquet and master more advanced skills and recipes. You may then choose to learn some Wealth Cooking specialties and accelerate your gourmet wealth life with property or equity investing or creating a business that will expand your wealth significantly.

Perhaps you'll discover you really love Wealth Cooking and being able to turn a few cents into a self-replenishing banquet. Having mastery over money and yourself, you'll see the endless possibilities this creates (as well as how much fun it is!) and you may even choose to master all the wealth specialties, becoming a Gourmet Wealth Chef.

Reading, learning, and mastering these Wealth Recipes will save you both time and money by learning from others' mistakes and successes. The recipes will show you how to create a steady stream of Income flowing into your life without having to swap time for money for the rest of your days.

Most important, these recipes will free up your mind from stress and worry, because once applied, your financial freedom will be assured.

Just like cooking

This book provides you with all the tools, skills, and knowledge you'll need to get your money and wealth sorted forever. It helps you to:

- Learn the basic Wealth Ingredients to use in your Wealth Cooking and how to combine them and use them to create your Financial Freedom Feast.

- Discover the kind of Wealth Cook you've been until now, and the type of Wealth Chef you need to become in order to achieve your own financial freedom.

- Determine exactly what financial freedom means for you and set a very clear target and intermediate milestones to get there.

- Start investing in wealth-generating Assets.

- Create a powerful Debt Destroyer Recipe, ensuring that worrying about debt becomes a thing of the past.

- Develop your own unique Financial Freedom Feast Menu, complete with the Wealth Recipes that you need to create it.

- Learn the core Wealth Recipes and practice the key Wealth Cooking skills needed to keep and grow your money.

- Know which insurance and key wealth documents you need in your life so you can have greater confidence that you and those you love are protected.

- Learn accelerated Wealth Cooking specialties and advanced Wealth Cooking techniques that you can use to take your Wealth Cooking to a gourmet level— and so achieve financial abundance.

Just like cooking, you'll discover there are many ways to create wealth, as well as many wealth-generating specialties, but to succeed at any of them, you must master the five core recipes of wealth, understand how the key ingredients work, and be familiar with the characteristics and skills of successful Wealth Chefs. In the kitchen, I doubt that we would attempt to make a soufflé if we hadn't yet learned how to separate an egg!

Just as in cooking, wealth skills are built upon, one step at a time. The Wealth Chef is structured to teach you all the ingredients, skills, and recipes you'll need, in the order in which you'll need them. Learn them, apply them, and master them and your financial freedom will be assured.

You've already taken the biggest step

By the end of this content-packed book, you'll know and understand the fundamental tools, processes, ingredients, and Wealth Recipes, so that you, too, can create your feast and achieve financial freedom.

Including:
- 6 Wealth Pots
- 5 Core Wealth Recipes
- 5 Wealth Cooking Tools
- 4 Fundamental Wealth Flavors
- 4 Asset Groups
- 2 Wealth Spices
- 1 Wealth Accelerator
- 1 Unique Financial Freedom Feast Menu

Once you know and understand these tools and recipes, and apply them in your life, you'll find wealth creation is as easy as boiling an egg!

This book isn't a get-rich-quick scheme. Becoming financially free is not difficult but it does require a tremendous commitment. Like any worthwhile goal, it requires time, effort, discipline, and an open mind. But believe me, not achieving financial freedom is a far greater burden! Never mastering your money nor achieving financial freedom will suck energy, enjoyment, and pleasure out of your life, as well as prevent you from living the life that you're born to live!

My goal is for you to learn from my own and other peoples' mistakes, so that your path to financial freedom can be even quicker than mine. With the recipes and the clear step-by-step approach provided in this book, I know you can achieve all of your financial dreams.

So let's get cooking!

You've already taken the biggest step on your financial freedom journey: you've made a decision. You've decided to master money, you've chosen wealth, and you've taken action by purchasing this book.

This alone is a huge step that most people won't make because they've decided wealth isn't meant for them— it's too hard or too complicated, they're too young or too old, or a litany of other excuses.

Set yourself up for success

This is an intensive program, and a significant amount of content and information will be covered. Please prepare yourself for this upfront, and give yourself the gift of making space in your life to put the time in, not just to read the content but also to complete the exercises.

You may find resistance to doing this and feel what I call MMAB (Money Management Avoidance Behavior) coming up in you. Nothing to worry about: this is a completely normal reaction when we decide to make any changes from our usual way of doing things.

If you find yourself MMABing—perhaps mopping the floor suddenly feels more fun than getting your money paperwork out—then just observe your reaction, smile, and get on with doing what you need to do. The floor can wait, your wealth can't!

Before we start, make sure your Wealth Kitchen is set up to support you.

Buy a file in which to keep your worksheets and notes, as well as the information that you'll be downloading from the Wealth Chef website (see the link at the end of book).

I also encourage you to keep a Wealth Journal. This is separate from the notes that you'll be taking. It's where you'll track your emotional wealth journey, jotting down your key learnings and keeping a record of what comes up for you as you work through this book and beyond, as your mind and reality shifts to allow wealth in. I also recommend keeping a note of each and every wealth success you create! This is so important, as energy flows where focus goes and this journal will be a key tool in helping you keep your focus on wealth!

You've already made a commitment to read this book, a commitment of both time and money. So, commit now to getting massive value out of it by following through, completing each and every exercise, and implementing the recipes and skills in your life. Only through action, your action, can you create change.

Why? Because you're worth it.

With love,
Ann Wilson

2.

My Story

My name is Ann—Ann Wilson. I was born in South Africa, a twin and the fifth of six children, so I learned how to enjoy hand-me-downs and make myself heard.

After studying civil engineering, and armed with additional business management studies, I worked all over the world on exciting infrastructure projects, not only playing with big construction toys but also having the privilege of adding value and creating Assets that helped improve people's lives.

Along the way, I met my husband, and together we've lived and worked in Hong Kong, Australia, London, South Africa, and now Paris.

From my last corporate role as general manager of contracts and procurement for a huge infrastructure delivery program in South Africa (where I was responsible for making sure $12 billion was spent effectively on infrastructure delivery), I now spend my time doing what I love most: walking my dog in beautiful places and teaching others the recipes for wealth so they, too, can be free to live their lives on their terms.

My journey to financial freedom wasn't always smooth. But put away the violins! If you're expecting a rags-to-riches story or perhaps some cataclysmic event where I saw the light and everything changed in my life, I'm sorry to disappoint you. I didn't end up living in a container next to the highway, I've never starved, and I haven't had a near-death experience (yet!).

❖

I grew up in a nice home, on an average street, with nice average siblings. (Well . . . not really—we seemed to spend a lot of time in emergency rooms with one or another of the kids being stitched up!) My mum was a housewife and my father worked exceptionally hard trying to provide for his horde. I received a good education and I had good opportunities.

I was lucky: when I was 16 years old, I wandered into my dad's office while he was poring over stocks and share prices in the newspaper (yes, back then that's how it was done!) and asked him what he was doing. He explained to me a little about buying and selling shares and that he was investing in our financial future—I really don't remember much of the details, but what stayed with me was the following: "Ann," he said, "you are the only person who can ever truly look after your own financial well-being. You must take responsibility for your own financial future; you can't blindly hope that a pension, a husband, a job, or the government will ever do this for you: only you can make sure you have your wealth sorted out, and it's your responsibility, alone."

I say I'm lucky, because my father planted a seed in me—a seed that took root, germinated, and then just grew and grew!

The problem, however, was that learning about money and actually doing what he said I should do was the furthest thing from my mind and so I happily romped through the next few years, having a ball, believing (like most people) that "tomorrow is another day." "I've got time to learn later," I used to say to myself. "When I've got money, when I'm older . . ."

Fortunately, my father walked his talk and was a great provider.

Unfortunately, he died young, leaving my mom a widow and literally clueless when it came to managing money. Dad had always taken care of that.

My father had set things up so that my mom was comfortably off financially; sadly, though—knowing what I know now—she never had the skills to keep growing the money that she'd been left, and although it saw her through for the next twenty-plus years, she had to be financially careful in the last few years of her life.

Even so, she was significantly better off than most of her friends.

Here's the thing: 90 percent of all women will have to manage their own money and financial well-being at some stage of their lives, yet the vast majority of these women won't have a clue how to do it!

❖

Let's look at some numbers:

- Women are marrying later: in the United States, at 26.5, in the United Kingdom at 28.5, in Australia, at 27.5, and in South Africa, at 27 years old.

- One in every three marriages ends in divorce (one in two, in some places).

- Even if a woman remarries, she'll typically spend around three years on her own between marriages.

- About 30 percent of women never marry.

- In the Anglo-Saxon world, nearly one in three children are born outside traditional marriage.

- Only around 22 percent of women die while married, due to longer life expectancy for women.

If we look at the cumulative impact of those statistics, we'll quickly realize that at some point in their lives, 90 percent of women will have to take responsibility for their own financial well-being. But—and this is a very large "but!"—it's just not something that we've been taught.

And what about men? Our society still thinks it's the man's role to "look after" the money, but . . . who taught the men? They receive the same education as women but have to pretend that they actually know what's going on. Heaven forbid the poor guy who confesses to total ignorance! No wonder money is cited as the number one cause of conflict in most marriages.

❖

I was just 22 when my dad died—never having learned how to manage, invest, or grow money from the only source I knew who knew how. With a hunger for knowledge and my father's voice in my ear telling me I had to take responsibility for my own financial well-being, I started out on my wealth journey.

I started with the only recipe I knew: that of getting a good job, working hard, and hoping like hell that there would be something left at the end of it all!

So I got stuck in; I studied hard (with a few detours!) to get a good job, worked hard to earn money, and then spent it on loads of stuff because—well, that's just what you do, isn't it?

When I got my first job after graduation, I was suddenly being offered money all round—store cards, credit cards, overdrafts for all the things a professional "needs." "Why wait?" I was told. I not only could have it all now, but I actually had to have it now in order to be someone, to fit in, to be respected and successful—and, after all, I would be making good money, so I could pay for it later. In any case—that insidious phrase—I was "worth it."

So that's exactly what I did: I got the credit cards, opened the store cards, took out an overdraft, and even got an additional bank loan to buy a red white-water rafting kayak, because I'd decided that would be a fun thing to do. Yes, I went into debt to buy a red plastic boat! Two months' salary's worth!

I then bought an apartment with an enormous mortgage and filled it with furniture bought on credit from the furniture store.

Then I met a man. He wined and dined and courted me, and I needed nicer clothes to make sure I looked fab—luckily, I had the store cards for all that! We went on wonderful holidays (all on credit cards), impressing each other and, being suitably impressed, we decided to get married.

As we were bringing our lives together, I discovered he was even better at this credit business than me. The only problem was that nobody had actually ever told him he was meant to pay off his credit cards! But, hey, that's what love is all about, isn't it? I quickly helped him out by putting some of his debt onto my cards, and off we set again to do what we were meant to do: industriously ticking all the boxes—the box of a nicer car to go with the nice new marriage (with a bigger car loan), a larger and better house to go with the car (with an even larger mortgage), brand-new furniture to go with the new house, to go with the new car, to match the nice new marriage (all of these on store credit—apart from the marriage!). And all so that we could fit in and follow the "script."

Luckily, in my late twenties, I stepped back and took a long, hard look at where I was headed, and I didn't like what I saw. I suddenly saw all the "stuff" that we'd accumulated for exactly what it was: an enormous burden.

I felt suffocated and terrified that this was going to be my life: a life spent paying for stuff, over and over again, long after any pleasure of buying it had dissipated. Worse still, I saw a life of stifled mediocrity, of being held back by this burden, of being unable to do the things I wanted to do because I'd dug a hole too deep to get out of.

I remember reading a quote at that time, which said, "If you're in a hole that you want to get out of, the first thing you need to do is stop digging."

I also saw my dad's face. I'd been blessed to spend quite a lot of time with him in his last few months, and during that time, as he was dying, he had told me to make sure my life meant something. He'd told me to live my life with passion and adventure and that, at the end of the day, what would matter would be whether I could look back and know that I'd experienced a full life, that I'd given myself fully to it—a life where I'd spread my wings, where I'd pushed myself, where I'd really lived on my terms and, most important, where I'd fulfilled my purpose.

And yet here I was, only a few years after he'd died, heading down a completely different path, defined by someone else, locking myself into a prison of debt, just to fit into a definition of success that certainly didn't make my soul sing! I realized that I was incredibly lucky, however, because, although we'd managed to build up a significant pile of debt—more than a year's worth of salary—we could change how this story was going to end.

By using the steps and strategies you'll learn in this book, we were able to get rid of all our consumer debt in six months—which also included getting rid of a great deal of "stuff." We became great salespeople!

As we saw the benefit of having fewer belongings and our debt reducing rapidly, we got so much into clearing everything out that we ended up with enough money to backpack around the world for a year without having to work.

And that's exactly what we did!

I can honestly say that the lessons I learned in that time set me up for my subsequent journey to financial freedom and my wealth success.

I'd learned the first key wealth skill: how to spend less than I earned, and to save. I'd also discovered a key element of Wealth Recipe #1: pay yourself first.

After a year of traveling, and mastering how to live on very little, I got a job in Hong Kong. We arrived in Hong Kong after having traveled down the River Yangtze, and I just thought: wow, this city's cool, I'd love to work here for a while! So I did.

This was the start of the second leg of my wealth journey. I felt I had to master what my dad had told me about making sure I looked after my own financial future, and so I implemented the next part of the recipe that I'd learned up till then: stay out of debt, spend as little as possible, and save, save, save! I got this formula down pat, in the process developing what I now realize is a money disorder: Money Anorexia. I believed I needed to control money to feel safe.

I'd gone from one extreme to another, spending as little as I could, believing that if I did this, one day I'd be able to live the life I truly wanted. I needed to see how little I could live on. I was so tightly in control, that I managed to make my husband and I live on less than 20 percent of what we earned, investing and saving over 80 percent of our combined incomes. And this in Hong Kong, which isn't exactly the cheapest place on the planet!

Wow, you may think, awesome! Yes, it was, but it also came with a truckload of fear, deprivation, over-control, and meanness. You see, I also had a whole bunch of confused beliefs about money: I wanted money but felt guilty about having it—so, in order to have it, I had better not enjoy it too much!

Looking back, I now understand what happened: I thought I controlled money and held on very tightly, but I didn't, in reality, understand it. I had no idea that money needed to flow and move. I also wasn't letting myself play and be creative. I made having money not fun.

And then, the only thing that could happen, happened: my whole life blew up in a spectacular way, and I ended up losing both my marriage and the money that I'd held on to so tightly.

I clearly remember, the Tuesday afternoon my husband left, sobbing on the bathroom floor of my tiny apartment in Hong Kong, feeling lost, confused, angry, and incredibly lonely, not knowing where to go or what to do. What was I meant to do now—because, obviously, what I'd been doing up till then hadn't worked?

The following hours and days I devoted to reflecting on my situation. I realized that although I knew how to save money, I didn't have a clue about how money worked and that just "not spending it" wasn't enough to be wealthy.

I also realized that having money and financial freedom was not an end in itself—it was a very, very important means, but not the end. I also wanted a life—adventure, experience, joy, and relationships. In other words, I wanted to be wealthy and not just have a great deal of money. There is a difference.

And so started the third leg of my wealth education journey: my journey to financial freedom and true wealth.

❖

It wasn't simple—far from it! Though I really wanted to get this wealth business sorted, I didn't know where to focus. Where to start? This just wasn't being taught in a straightforward way. I found inspirational books that got me all revved up but didn't tell me how to do it, as they weren't action oriented; I found deathly dry investment books that put me to sleep before I got past page ten; I found books on debt, or on property, but nowhere was everything put together in a simple, straightforward way, inspiring practical action.

The good news is that through all those experiences, I never gave up! I held steadfastly to the belief that it is possible to learn to be wealthy.

I studied hundreds of books, attended seminars and trainings, tried numerous different investment strategies, and through all this, I discovered that there were actually only a handful of core recipes for wealth, which if learned and consistently applied would lead me to financial freedom while I lived my life fully—while I lived my life, on my terms and using my definition of value.

And as soon as I decided to master these simple core recipes and stick to them, financial freedom came very quickly.

I also discovered who I needed to become and what I needed to believe about money to not only create wealth but to keep it and grow it, too. Most important, I realized I could have both—a rich, full life, while keeping and growing my money and become financially free. In other words, I discovered the recipe for wealth!

It took me only eight years from that Tuesday afternoon to become financially free. Along the way, I made sure that this time I enjoyed the journey and really experienced wealth: I traveled around Australia for three months on a motorbike; renovated three homes (always adding value), learning to make lead light windows and Tiffany lamps because one of the houses needed them; I lived in Australia, the United Kingdom, and the United States, and went back to South Africa and then to Paris; I became a fire-walking instructor, NLP master practitioner and trainer; I got my motorbike license, hot-air ballooned over Palm Springs and the plains of Africa; white-water rafted down the massive Zambezi River, and canoed through the Okavongo Delta.

I bungee jumped off the Victoria Falls Bridge, worked on property developments with my brother and built a magnificent home that was featured in one of South Africa's premier home magazines, spent time with chimpanzees, dived in the Red Sea, skied and sailed all over the world, and at the same time worked full-time and had an incredibly successful career.

During this entire time, I kept applying the core recipes: spending less than I earned, always paying myself first, and consistently growing my wealth. I found that by putting a strong financial foundation in my life and just applying these core recipes over and over again while I focused on doing my best in each area of my life, with passion and joy, wealth would flow in. And it still does!

I'm sharing this with you not to brag but to hopefully inspire you to realize that financial freedom is possible for you, too. It is possible to live life to the fullest and have loads of amazing experiences while creating your financial freedom!

I don't know where you are in your wealth journey right now. Perhaps you're just starting out and don't have a clue where to begin? Perhaps you've been earning money for a while now, but whenever you try to figure it all out, you have more incomprehensible jargon thrown at you—or, worse, some broker trying to sell you yet another financial product designed to make him rich?

Maybe you have some investments but you've outsourced your freedom, and you've handed it all over to a financial planner—preferring to let them handle that "stuff." Maybe you've also tried a whole bunch of wealth creation quick-fixes, only to end up back where you started?

Or are you just tired of stressing about your financial future, worrying about debts and having enough money to educate your children, and just plain sick of wondering how you will ever get to grips with your money.

Wherever you are right now, you're in the right place! The Wealth Chef will show you the big picture, lifting the fog for you and showing you how to make money, and wealth, an integral part of your life—finally.

3.

Wealth Cooking: The Fundamentals

Understanding the fundamentals of Wealth Cooking was pivotal to my achieving financial freedom. Before I truly got these concepts, I was making loads of money actions, I was focusing on increasing my Income, and I was even investing, but I didn't understand these fundamentals and how they worked together, and so my wealth never grew.

Quite frankly, I looked like an octopus on roller skates! There was a lot of action happening but I was getting absolutely nowhere. Once I fully grasped these concepts, though, my journey to financial freedom accelerated rapidly—and now, I'm happy to say, I get to live my life fully on my terms.

And so can you!

There are four sets of fundamentals you need to understand in order to be a great Wealth Cook: Wealth Flavors, Wealth Flows, Wealth Ingredients, and Wealth Spices.

So, now, roll up your sleeves and let's get down to it!

The Four Wealth Flavors

Just like food has four-plus-one basic tastes—sweet, bitter, sour, and salty, plus umami (savory)—so wealth has four basic flavors. The very first thing to learn is how to tell one from the other, as success with your Wealth Feast depends on how well you use them and combine them in your Wealth Cooking.

As with cooking, you can have great ingredients to work with, but if you don't understand flavors and just throw your ingredients in together without any understanding of how they affect your dish or how they interact with one another, you'll just end up with an inedible mess.

Knowing these flavors is absolutely vital, so we're going to make sure you grasp them fully.

Let me introduce you to the stars of the show. The Four Wealth Flavors are:

- Assets
- Liabilities
- Income
- Expenditure

We need to know the difference between an Asset and a Liability, and between Income and Expenditure. Wealth Cooking is about buying Assets and stocking them in your Wealth Pantry. It's that simple.

Unfortunately, simple isn't always easy. Most people have never learned what an Asset is and never get to truly know the difference between an Asset and a

Liability. Even our banks and the financial planning industry don't understand the difference when it comes to creating wealth. And understanding the difference is key to being wealthy.

Wikipedia defines an Asset as "Money and other valuables belonging to an individual or business." It also defines Liabilities as "A type of borrowing from persons or banks that is payable during a short or long time." No wonder people get confused! When I hear some of that financial talk, my eyelids begin to close. Is it the same for you?

Don't worry: you don't have to talk like that to be great at Wealth Cooking!

Banks define Assets as "Anything you own that can be sold and converted to cash." In terms of creating your Wealth Feast, thinking an Asset is anything that you can sell and convert to cash is not only wrong, but it's downright dangerous.

What defines something as an Asset is not words, but numbers.

Now, stop!

If you're freaking out because I've mentioned that seven-letter "N" word, numbers, here's the deal:

You'll never be able to create wealth if you don't understand numbers. You don't need to learn complex equations and calculus, but you must train yourself to understand how Wealth Flows—and to do this, you need to be able to recognize the patterns that money makes as it moves through your life, and you do this by looking at the numbers. If you can't read the numbers, you'll never be able to recognize the wealth flow patterns and know whether you're filling your life with Assets or Liabilities.

But here's the good news: it's not difficult!

So often people come up to me and say, "Oh, Ann, I've just bought a great property!" They give me some numbers, and without their even having to go into any detail, I can feel my toenails starting to curl because I realize they have no idea how to recognize the wealth flow pattern and so they can't tell an Asset from a Liability—yes, they've bought property, but it's not an Asset. They're unable to recognize the flow of wealth that the numbers are telling them—a flow straight out of their lives.

The Wealth Pantry

Illustration 1 shows the two compartments of your Wealth Pantry, each with two drawers in which to keep your Wealth Cooking Flavors.

The Income Statement compartment holds your Income and your Expenditure. The Balance Sheet compartment holds your Assets and your Liabilities.

So what actually is an Asset and what is a Liability?

In terms of Wealth Cooking, the simplest way to differentiate them is as follows:

An Asset is something that causes money to flow back into your life.

A Liability is something that causes money to flow out of your life.

It's as simple as that. To create wealth, you need to stock up your Asset Drawer. If you want to be poor, spend your life filling up your Liability Drawer.

Many novice Money Cooks don't understand the relationship between the two compartments and the flavors stored in them. Understanding the relationship between the flavors and between the compartments is vital to becoming a successful Wealth Chef and achieving financial freedom. Not understanding it is the primary cause of financial struggle.

WEALTH COOKING FLAVORS

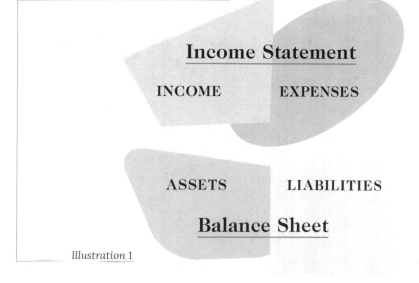

Income Statement

INCOME   EXPENSES

ASSETS   LIABILITIES

Balance Sheet

Illustration 1

The Wealth Flows

To grasp the difference between an Asset and a Liability, you need to understand Wealth Flows.

Wealth Flows are the patterns that money creates, depending on the flavors you use in your Wealth Cooking.

Each flavor has its own Wealth Flow. Income brings wealth flowing into your life. Expenses cause wealth to flow out of your life. An Asset feeds your wealth by causing money to flow back into your life in the form of Income, whereas a Liability withers your wealth by causing money to flow out of your life through your Expenses.

Illustration 2 shows the Wealth Flow pattern of an Asset. Illustration 3 shows the Wealth Flow pattern of a Liability.

It's not just the individual flavors that have unique Wealth Flows. When flavors are combined in different ways and in different quantities, different Wealth Flow patterns emerge. To understand this better, let's look at the Wealth Flow patterns created by different Money Cook types.

Illustration 4 shows the Wealth Flow of Break-even Money Cooks. Their Asset and Liability Drawers are empty. All the Income that flows into the Income Statement compartment is consumed by their Expenses.

These Money Cooks are those who have no access to credit, typically youngsters and students and many people who either have destroyed their ability to

ASSETS WEALTH FLOW

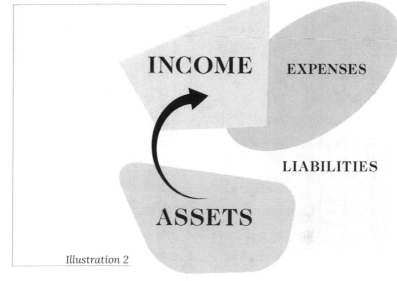

Illustration 2

LIABILITIES WEALTH FLOW

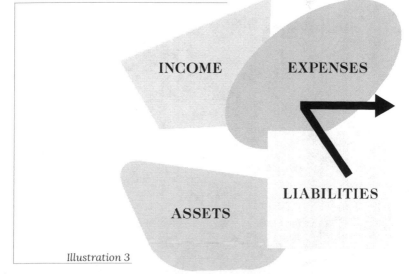

Illustration 3

access credit or are fearful of debt. These people lead completely break-even lives. All the Income that comes into their lives goes flowing straight out in Expenses— and if the flow of Income increases, so does the outflow via Expenses.

The Break-evens live their financial life hand-to-mouth: money comes in, money goes out. They've never been taught that they can actually keep some of what they make!

When the money ends before the month ends, they starve. Break-evens have no concept of Net Worth, having no Assets, no Liabilities, and no Balance Sheet to speak of. Break-evens believe their problem is their Income. They believe that if they just made more money, then they'd be okay.

BREAK-EVEN MONEY FLOW

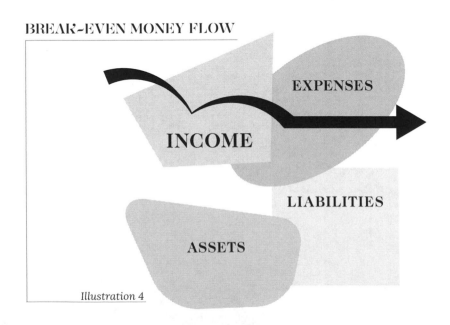

Illustration 4

Looking at illustration 4, you'll notice that their wealth flow completely bypasses their Asset and Liability Drawers. They don't know these flavors exist. In fact, most Break-even Money Cooks don't even know that the Balance Sheet compartment in their Wealth Pantry exists!

This brings me to the second type: the Spend Everything and Borrow More Money Cook.

Borrow Mores have the worst wealth flow of any other Money Cook, including the Break-evens. They have most certainly discovered the second Wealth Cooking compartment, specifically the Liability Drawer. They have very high consumer debt and an ever-expanding Liability Drawer that pumps the wealth out of their lives faster and faster.

SPEND EVERYTHING AND
BORROW MORE MONEY FLOW

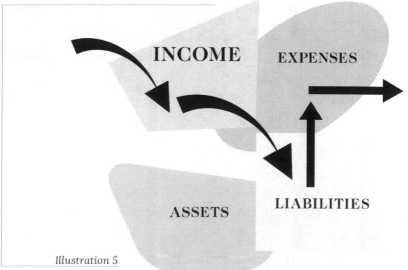

Illustration 5

They spend all they make, and borrow more. With the Spend Everything and Borrow More Money Cooks, Income flows straight into the Liabilities Drawer. They fill up their Wealth Pantry with lots of Liabilities, usually basing their purchase decisions on nothing more than whether they can afford the monthly repayment, which, in turn, increases their Expenses—and so all the money flows out of their life again and again.

This is the Wealth Flow pattern of the Buy Now—Pay Later culture, where people live "on credit." Borrow Mores have bought into the illusion that having things equals wealth.

Borrow Mores also believe that Income is the answer to their problems. One day they'll earn more, they think, and then they'll pay off their debt. They refuse to see that the problem isn't their Income, but what they do with it and the wealth flow pattern they're creating as a result.

This is the wealth flow pattern of the TV Dinner Money Cooks. They represent a large proportion of the middle classes in Western societies. A small amount of their Income trickles down into their Asset Drawer, but most of it pours out of the Expense Drawer, pumped out by their Liabilities.

As Income comes in, they—like the Spend Everything and Borrow Mores—buy a whole bunch of Liabilties and because they don't understand Wealth Flows, they often believe they're buying Assets. They typically own a big house and a fancy car (which increase their Expenses and so money flows out of their lives), but they've understood that they need to save a little here or invest a little there, so a small amount of money also trickles into their Asset Drawer.

TV Dinner Money Cooks are aware of the need to save and invest. They often have some sort of retirement plan that they contribute to, and some even have additional investments in some form of equity-based packaged investment product. But they prefer others to take responsibility for their Wealth Feast. They want to eat well, but aren't prepared to learn how to cook. They usually buy prepacked TV dinner investment products at high costs, and often the amount diverted into their Asset Drawer isn't really enough to make any sort of difference to their lives.

TV DINNER
MIDDLE-CLASS MONEY FLOW

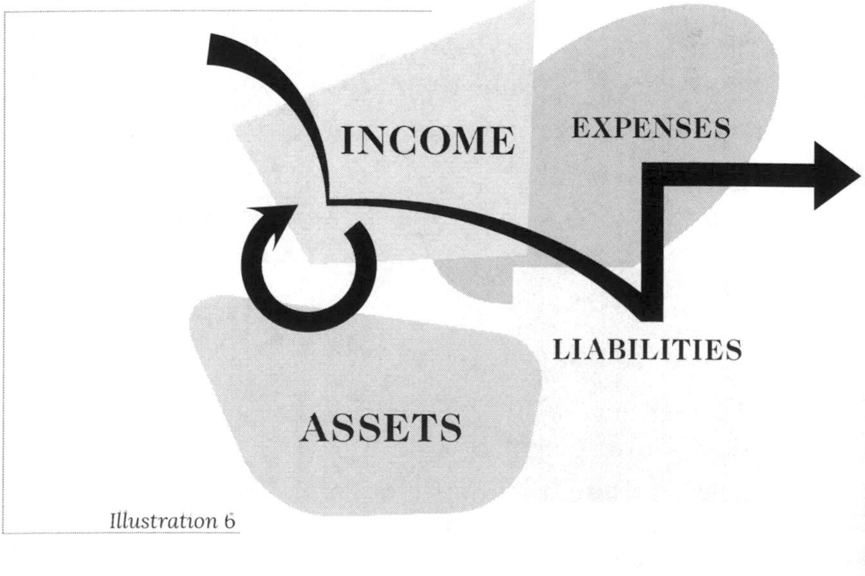

INCOME   EXPENSES

LIABILITIES

ASSETS

Illustration 6

The final flow is the Wealth Flow of Wealth Chefs. They use Income to buy Assets, which in turn pour Income back into their Income Drawer, and that then pays for their Expenses. Hold the image in your mind. This is the Wealth Flow pattern that we're aiming for!

The previous illustrations are all, obviously, simplified. They show the flow of wealth through the hands of a variety of Money Cook types, as well as the flow caused by the use of different Wealth Flavors. They are useful because once we understand these dynamics, we understand how to change the flow.

These illustrations also clearly show why Income is not the most important flavor in Wealth Cooking! I'm going to repeat that because it's so important: **Income is not the most important flavor—Assets are.**

This is important. Most people focus on trying to increase their Income, believing this will solve their problems. But having more money won't solve their Wealth Flow problem—in fact, it may exacerbate it. Money is energy and energy is a magnifier. If you add energy to something that is fundamentally flawed, all you do is magnify the flaw. If more Income flows into a flawed Wealth Flow pattern, in most cases it just causes the faulty pattern to flow even faster! It doesn't change the pattern. Only you can change the pattern: until you manage to transform your Wealth Flow pattern into a healthy one, having more Income is just not going to solve your problems.

This is why, all too often, when a person who isn't a Wealth Chef has a windfall (such as winning the lottery or coming into a large inheritance), the money flows out of their life incredibly quickly and they end up losing all the money and returning to the same financial mess as before—or worse. If your pattern is one of spending everything you get—money flowing into the Income Drawer and then straight out of the Expenses Drawer again—an increase in Income will just result in an increase in spending.

Most of us are never taught the difference between the Four Wealth Flavors. The only "recipe" we know is to get a good job and focus our whole lives on working harder and earning more—that is, to increase our Income. We only ever learn the flavors of Income, Expenses, and Liabilities but never learn the key flavor—

**THE WEALTH CHEF
MONEY FLOW**

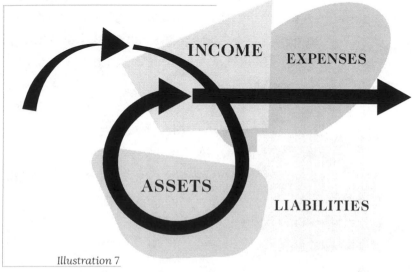

Illustration 7

Assets. We learn a recipe to work hard for money, but only a few ever learn the recipe to get money to work hard for us!

The Asset Drawer is the only place where money can work for you and Assets are the only flavor that expands wealth. If money is not in your Asset Drawer in the form of Assets, it can't do what it's meant to do. And money is meant to grow.

Start noticing the patterns you've made with your money in the past and how it's been flowing in your life. The more you can notice this flow and identify the different Wealth Flavors and whether something is an Asset or a Liability, the quicker your journey to financial freedom will be. Keep asking yourself whenever you're about to buy something: "Is this going to cause more money to flow out of my life or into my life?"

Money has power. Sadly, most people allow the power of money to control them—to work against them. These are the same people who say, "Money isn't important," but who get up every day, work hard for their money to get it to flow into their lives . . . and then let it all pour out of their Expenses Drawer, pumped out by Liabilities. They work for everyone except themselves.

They work for the owner of the company where they work, they work for the bank to pay off their mortgage and loans, and they work for the government, giving the taxman the first four or five months of their earnings every year.

They then work for the retailers, giving them whatever money is left over, for a whole bunch of stuff that they don't need. It does look like slavery!

Understand this: if you don't have control over the flow of your money, money has control over you!

The Asset Drawer

As you've already discovered, an Asset is something that makes money flow back into your life.

So is your house an Asset? The bank will tell you it is; your financial planner will tell you it is. I'm telling you that your home is a Liability.

Owning your own home is for many people their dream, as well as their biggest investment. I own my own home, and having a home without a mortgage is a wonderful place to be. (I remember distinctly the day when the mortgage on my primary residence was paid off!) Knowing that you have a place that is wholly yours is a fantastic feeling, and I really encourage people to own their own homes—but don't be fooled into believing that your home is an Asset!

As long as you live in your home, as long as you're paying rates and taxes on it, as well as a mortgage and home insurance, and you're also paying to maintain it, and aren't receiving any Income from it, it's a Liability. It's making money flow out of your life.

Is your car an Asset? Nope, it's a big Liability. As soon as you purchase a car, it loses value. And on top of that, it costs you money. It causes money to flow out of your life. You pay to keep it licensed, you pay to maintain it, and you pay for insurance on it. It's a Liability.

Most people never understand the difference between an Asset and a Liability and so spend their lives buying Liabilities, mistakenly thinking they're Assets. They buy a bigger house, believing they now have a larger Asset and are wealthier. In fact, all they've done is fill up their Liability and Expenses Drawer.

Their mortgage goes up, the insurance goes up, the rates and taxes go up, and the maintenance also goes up. So they focus on increasing their Income to pay for all these Expenses—and the Wealth Flow pattern stays the same, just going faster.

The same happens if they buy a new, more expensive car, believing that this will also make them wealthy. Again, all that happens is that they increase their Liabilities and Expenses. Their car tax goes up, their insurance goes up, and their maintenance goes up.

I was horrified the other day when I heard someone describing her $1,000 shoes as an Asset. No, darling, all you have is yet another expensive thing cluttering your life, which has just killed a whole bunch of your little wealth elves, who could have been beavering away creating more money for you!

So, sadly, these people lose more than just the money they spend on Liabilities: they also lose the money they have to spend to maintain them. The biggest loss of all, however, is the loss of all the opportunities that they missed to buy Assets—real Assets. You see, if all of your

Income is tied up maintaining an expensive lifestyle and feeding your Liabilities, you can't add to your Asset Drawer—and Asset is the only flavor that creates wealth.

So, what should you be stocking in your Asset Drawer?

Asset ingredients fall into four groups:

1. **Equity:** stocks and shares, bonds and mutual funds. In essence, they are a part of "another business"—you share in the profits of somebody else's business. The Income from equities is sometimes called portfolio income.

2. **Income-generating property:** residential or commercial. This is not your private home. These are properties from which you receive Income in the form of rent. Income from property is sometimes called passive income.

3. **Low-input businesses:** businesses that make a profit for you, without your having to be actively involved. They include royalties from books, e-products, patents, and music. These are things that keep bringing money into your life—businesses where you put the effort in upfront and then leave them to do what they're meant to do, which is to make you money. They also include vending machines, ATMs, automatic car wash systems, and most online businesses, which, once created, are driven and sold through a series of automated systems.

4. You: your mind and your ability to create value and grow your Income to feed your Asset Drawer.

But if Asset is the only flavor that actually creates wealth, what are the other flavors in the Wealth Pantry for? The answer is: they work together to create wealth.

Flavors work together

Just like in cooking, we need a mix of flavors. Wealth Flavors work in the same way as, say, salt—which we need in order to bring out some of the taste in life.

We all have Expenses, and always will. Expenses are about living and enjoying our life, and we need to enjoy it—but in a managed, conscious way. Consciously knowing that every bit of money we let flow out of our lives will bring value. We also need Liabilities. Liabilities are the fuel that gives us the initial boost on our wealth journey. When we use Liabilities with skill, we can really accelerate our wealth journey exponentially. This is the difference between good debts (which make our wealth grow) and bad debts (which destroy our wealth), and being able to read Wealth Flow patterns will help you recognize the difference.

We also need Income to cover our Expenses but, more important, we need it to fill our Asset Drawer. And we need Assets to feast on!

A healthy, abundant Wealth Flow uses all four flavors (Assets, Liabilities, Income, and Expenditure) in balance. You need to understand the relationship between them and the role they play in your Wealth Cooking, so that you can create your Financial Freedom Feast.

Your goal in stocking your Wealth Pantry and creating a healthy wealth flow pattern in your life is to:

- Divert as much of your Income as possible to your Asset Drawer

- Reduce your Expenses and make this drawer as small as possible

- Reduce your Liability Drawer

- Increase your Asset Drawer

Illustration 8 shows the Wealth Pantry of the poor. This is really a Wealth Destroyer's Pantry: as you can see, there's a small Income and Asset Drawer and a large Liability Drawer that pumps money out and enlarges the Expenses Drawer.

Illustration 9 is the Wealth Chef's Pantry. There's a large Income Drawer, a huge drawer full of growing Assets, and then smaller, reasonably sized Liabilities and Expenses Drawers.

REMEMBER

- There are two compartments in your Wealth Pantry, each with two drawers in which to keep your Wealth Cooking Ingredients, sorted into four flavors.

- The Income Statement compartment holds your Income and your Expenses. The Balance Sheet compartment holds your Assets and your Liabilities.

WEALTH DESTROYER'S PANTRY

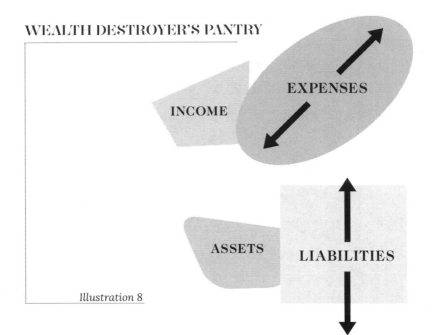

Illustration 8

WEALTH CHEF'S PANTRY

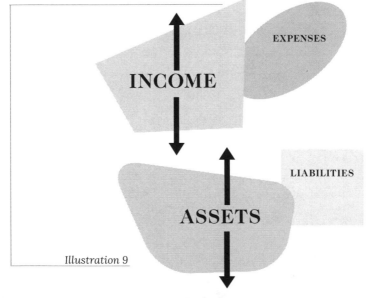

Illustration 9

Your life is your business. Your Income Statement, together with your Balance Sheet, are your two Wealth Cooking Measures that show you how successful you are in the money aspect of the business called your life. These are the most important performance measures you have to tell you how you're doing.

The Income Statement is also referred to as a profit and loss statement because it shows you whether you're making a profit or incurring a loss in your life—every month, every year. A business needs to make a profit or it very quickly ceases to exist. And the only way a business can make a profit is by ensuring that the Income going into the drawer in the Income Statement compartment is bigger than the Expenses going out!

The Balance Sheet compartment shows you whether your business—your wealth—is growing or shrinking. In nature, if something isn't growing, it's dying. You determine this by your Net Worth, which is simply the difference between the size of your Assets and Liabilities. Your goal is first, a positive Net Worth—that is, more Assets than Liabilities—and second, a positive Net Worth that is increasing! A Net Worth that doesn't increase every month is a clear sign of a sick Wealth Flow pattern, indicating that you need to change something fast!

For the benefit of your Wealth Cooking, the Income Statement and the Balance Sheet work together. The Balance Sheet adds to either the Income Drawer or the Expenses Drawer, depending on the size of the Asset and Liability columns. The more Assets you have in the

Balance Sheet, the more Income you have going into the Income Drawer—which means the more Assets you can buy—and so your wealth pot expands exponentially.

The more Liabilities you have, the more Expenses go into the Expenses Drawer—and so the less Income you have to buy Assets, which means your Wealth contracts and shrinks. It's as simple as that.

Illustration 10, the last, shows the full and complete wealth flow of a Master Wealth Chef.

A wealthy life (and healthy business) is one where the Income Statement and the Balance Sheet compartments are functioning with healthy Wealth Flow patterns—a big flow between your Income and your Asset Drawers, and a small flow between your Liabilities and your Expenses Drawer.

Your Wealth Cooking is a success when you're making a profit and when your Net Worth is increasing every month. If you aren't cooking a profit and growing your Net Worth, then something is wrong in your pantry!

Your Net Worth is the indicator of how far you've come in creating your wealth and how much you still need to cook before you can have your Financial Freedom Feast (which will feed you forever).

So from now on, your focus is going to move to your Net Worth as the most important indicator of how well you're doing in your Wealth Cooking.

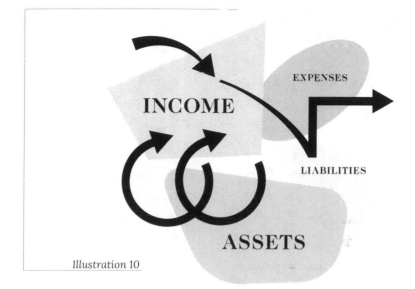

Illustration 10

Some things just have to be done!

I now want you to see exactly what's been happening with your Wealth Flows, what you've created with your money cooking, what kind of Money Cook you've been to date, and (more excitingly and importantly) what type of Wealth Chef you need to become to create the wealth patterns you want in your life. We're also going to be setting your very own wealth targets.

I know that for some of you, this next step will be one of the toughest on your whole wealth journey. But some things just have to be done, and the sooner we get them done, the better. It's a little like pulling off a Band-

Aid. We know it might hurt, so let's just rip it off and get it over and done with! I promise you: once you've got this part of your wealth journey sorted, you'll find the rest just gets easier and easier.

Remember a time when you were really enthusiastic about cooking something? For me, it usually means baking, a sort of domestic-goddess fantasy that I seem to have. I remember a time when I woke up with a real craving to make profiteroles—yes, those delicate puffy pastry balls filled with whipped cream and topped with chocolate ganache.

Imagine the scene: all fired up, you head to the kitchen, imagining how your family and friends are going to love these fabulous pastry puffs that you're about to create. First things first: the recipe. Now, you know you've seen a choux pastry recipe in a cookbook somewhere. Or was it online? You can't remember, so out all the books come and, as you rifle through one and then another without success, you start getting frustrated. Until, eventually, when you're almost ready to give up, you find the one you've been looking for.

But looking at the list of ingredients, you realize you need four eggs and you only have three. Off to the shops you go! The craving for profiteroles is diminishing rapidly, but you're a determined cook. So, back in the kitchen with the eggs, you finally get down to it. You measure out your ingredients and get the pastry going nicely. The eggs have been beaten in and your choux pastry has that shiny, smooth, silky texture it needs to be all ready to be piped onto your baking trays . . .

Oh, damn it, you've just remembered you have to pipe this blasted pastry! Where did your piping bag go? You rummage through your kitchen drawers, getting more irritated by the minute, reminding yourself why you don't bake—it's such a hassle! With no piping bag in sight, you fling open the trash can and throw the pastry away. Who wanted profiteroles anyway? They just make you fat!

There is nothing more frustrating in cooking than having a disorganized kitchen or a kitchen without the core utensils, equipment, or ingredients readily at hand. A well-structured kitchen, stocked with your core ingredients, the right pots and pans, appliances, and utensils, makes all the difference between a joyful cooking experience and one of complete and utter frustration.

The same goes for your Wealth Cooking. There are five key Wealth Cooking tools that you must have readily at hand—just these five and an organized kitchen and your Wealth Cooking will be a total pleasure!

Setting up the kitchen

You may find that the time spent initially developing your Wealth Cooking tools and organizing your Wealth Kitchen is a little tedious. But trust me on this: success or failure depends on how you set up your Wealth Kitchen now!

If your Wealth Kitchen is a complete shambles and you can't find the things you need when you need them, you'll just give up. Once you've set up your kitchen, though, maintaining it that way will be so much easier—and you'll find you can whizz around easily and effortlessly, knowing what is where and how to use it.

Later on in the book we'll be setting up a regular Money Date Night each month that you're going to have with your money and your wealth. This is a really fun night that you'll get excited about! This is the time during which you'll keep all of your Wealth Cooking tools updated and you'll track and see your progress.

Try to see this initial setup like one of those in-depth beauty sessions that you need after a long dry winter in order to get ready for the summer—you know the one: where you start the waxing, plucking, and tweezing; the facials; the hair treatments and colorings. This is what you're about to do now with your wealth measures. Not all of it feels good at the time, but the results sure are fabulous!

The five key Wealth Cooking tools

The five Wealth Cooking tools are:

1. Wealth Scales—Your Income Statement

2. Wealth Scales—Your Balance Sheet

3. Wealth Sieve—Your Big Why

4. Wealth Obsession Magnet—Your Financial
   Freedom Vision

5. Wealth Health Certificate –Your Credit Score

The first two Wealth Cooking tools are your Income Statement and your Balance Sheet. These are your Wealth Cooking Scales and they measure the state of your kitchen pantry. They tell you what your current "stock" levels are in each of the four Wealth Pantry drawers.

You can't change what you don't measure, and these two tools are your most critical wealth measurement tools. They tell you, in detail, your current balance—or lack thereof—of each flavor group and the type of ingredients you have in each pantry drawer. It is only with this information that you can see what ingredients you have to start with and where you need to make adjustments to create your own Financial Freedom Feast.

Maybe this will reveal my "inner geek," but I love the wealth measuring scales in my Wealth Kitchen so much that I actually have them on my computer desktop (and I update and manage them in just a few minutes, every time I need to—with some practice you will too).

In the next chapter, I'm going to help you create your own Income Statement and Balance Sheet—step by step.

To prepare for this, please start digging out everything that relates to your money. Get out all your bank statements, any loans or debts that you have, as well as pay slips or Income Statements from your business, if you're self-employed.

Also ask yourself the following questions:

- What is the money that flows into my life?

- What is the money that flows out of my life?

- What Liabilities do I have? (What do I owe?)

- What Assets do I own?

It's absolutely vital that you create your own Wealth Cooking Scales—in the form of your own Income Statement and Balance Sheet—before you move on to the next Financial Freedom Foundation step, which is all about seeing where you are now and where you need to get to, in order to be financially free. To do this, you'll need these two wealth measures.

Well done, you've now mastered the Wealth Flows!

You now understand the four Wealth Cooking flavors and how they work together to create either wealth heaven or money hell. You know how to recognize healthy Wealth Flows and you also know what you need to be creating in your own life.

4

Ingredients and Spices

John D. Rockefeller once said: "If you want to become wealthy, you must have your money work for you. The amount you get paid for your personal effort is relatively small compared with the amount you can earn by having your money make money."

Rockefeller was talking about an incredibly special Wealth Cooking additive, a yeast of sorts. Once you understand the Wealth Flavors and how this key additive, together with a few Wealth Cooking spices, works, Wealth Cooking magic starts to really sparkle! So before we go any further, I'd like to introduce you to the star additive in all of wealth creation.

Compounding

Imagine you're starting a new job and as you're negotiating your salary, you're offered the following:

"A dollar today, and then to double that each day for the next 30 days" or "$10,000 a day for the 30 days."

Which would you rather have?

If you chose the $10,000 a day, you'd have $300,000 by the end of the month—not bad. But if you did, then you most probably don't yet understand this ingredient and there is a strong chance that it's working against you and not for you.

If you chose a dollar that doubled each day for 30 days, well done! You'd have precisely $5,368,000 at the end of the 30 days. Yes! If you did choose this, then you may already have discovered the sexiest, most exciting wealth accelerator in the world. I'm talking about the yeast that is going to make your Wealth Feast cake grow and grow.

Einstein called it the Eighth, Natural Wonder of the World, banks and lenders love it, and wealthy people understand that it is the single most important element in their Wealth Pantry. So what is it?

It's called Compound Interest.

Compounding is where the money you earn from your money goes on to earn more money, without your doing anything, and so, accelerating your wealth significantly.

Compounding is also where you get charged interest on debts you owe; then interest gets charged on that interest, accelerating your debt into the stratosphere, making you very poor—and someone else very rich, at your expense.

In the Western world, average household debt sits at around 82 percent of household Income, and nearly a quarter of households struggle to keep up with the minimum repayments on their debt. These people sure do know compounding—it's working against them every day—but most of them don't understand it. When you truly understand compounding, you'll never again use credit to buy things, and you'll never ever again rob your investments! Compounding is the miracle element in your Wealth Pantry, the yeast that makes your money grow. But just like yeast, it needs to be left to do its job: it needs time and the right environment.

I love cooking, as you know by now, especially baking! Making bread is particularly cathartic and I just love the smell of freshly baked bread wafting through my home. Whenever I bake, I'm amazed and in awe at those tiny granules of yeast. When kick-started in the right way, incorporated into the flour, and then left to prove in a warm place, yeast goes ballistic. Doubling, quadrupling in size. But, if you prod it, poke it, fiddle with it, try to use the dough too soon, or put it in the wrong environment, it just dies and you end up with a rock-hard plank you could knock someone out with, rather than light, fluffy, satisfying bread!

This is exactly what compounding does to your money. (I love the fact that money is also sometimes referred to as dough—very apt!)

Just like yeast, compounding does its job no matter who uses it or when. It makes no value judgments; it will work for whoever's mastered it. It doesn't say, "Oh gee, this is a nice person, I'll wait till she has investments." Compounding will work against you if you're in debt, and work for you if you have investments: it's as simple as that.

Here's an example: if you leave $10 alone, invested at 10 percent for 10 years, it becomes $25.90—that is, two and a half times its original size, without any extra investment. In 200 years, that $10 compounded at 10 percent becomes $4.465 million, all by itself.

If this is the power of compounding, imagine the impact it will have on your wealth! Combining the power of compounding with regular investment contributions, adding in time, and leaving them alone in a conducive environment is what makes the magic work.

Okay, so you can probably manage a little more than $10, and you don't want to wait 200 years! If, from the day you start earning to the day you retire—let's say from age 18 to 65—you take just $250 a month and invest that in a low-cost fund returning a very achievable average return of 10 percent per annum, you'll be a dollar millionaire with $3,231,000 by retirement age. Better still, you would have only put in $141,000.

However, most people use compounding against themselves, when it should be working for them!

For those who need extra convincing: if you invest just 10 percent of your Income at an average market return during your entire working life, that money will make you twice as much money—yes, it will create twice as much money as you earn in your entire working career. How mind-blowing is that? That measly little 10 percent goes to work, like the elves helping the shoemaker, and ends up making twice the money you do!

Better still, it doesn't need a house; it doesn't need a cell phone or fancy wardrobe. It doesn't need anything, except your guidance and to be left alone in a lovely wealth-producing environment in your Asset Drawer!

Time

"Tomorrow is another day." "One day when I have some money to spare, I'll start investing." "One day I'll get a salary raise and pay off my debt." This is the chatter of money cooks who haven't yet understood how to deal with a key factor in cooking: time (and they certainly don't understand compounding either!).

Time is one of two vital Wealth Cooking spices that compounding needs to create its magic. Wealth Chefs understand that time is what feeds and nurtures their Wealth Cooking, enabling compounding and the other ingredients to work their wealth magic. Each and every day wasted on not investing will cost you dearly. Not only will it cost you in terms of the lost impact of compounding, but you'll also lose the most important thing of all: the opportunity to learn from experience. You gain experience as an investor by actually being in the game. The sooner you start gaining your 10,000 hours of investor experience, the sooner you'll have this investing business figured out, receiving sophisticated investor returns of 20 percent, 30 percent, and 50 percent, and so accelerating your wealth exponentially.

Let's go back to the example of the $250 invested each month: if you decided to wait 17 years until you were 35 before you started investing your $250 (after all, you're still young), at retirement you would have only $570,000. That's a huge $2,661,000 "lost." It's time that makes the difference. The longer you wait, the harder it will be for you to become wealthy. The difficulty becomes exponential too, like compounding in reverse. Get as much time as you can into your Wealth Pantry and let it start working its money magic right now!

Didn't I tell you that Wealth Cooking was simple?!

The rate of return

The second key Wealth Cooking spice is the rate of return or interest rate.

The rate of return or interest rate determines how hard your money is working for you.

This is like the heat you add to your cooking and how high you turn this up will determine how fast your feast gets cooked.

The rate of return is the percentage increase or loss of an investment or debt over a period of time. Rate of return is often expressed as an annual percentage; for example, an annual rate of return of 5 percent means the investment gained 5 percent over a 12-month period. An interest rate of 5 percent on any debt you owe means that the debt will increase by 5 percent over a 12-month period if you don't pay any of it off.

Back to our $250 invested each month: if you decide to learn how money works and to take a more active role in your investing, thereby achieving a higher rate of return than the market average, let's see what would happen.

Say you achieve just 1 percent more than the market average and receive an average 11 percent rate of return on your investment. At retirement you would have $4,701,000. That's a huge $1,500,000 gained for no extra money put in!

Now let's say you fail to achieve the market average return over time and only receive an average rate of return of 9 percent—just 1 percent less than the market average. At retirement you'd only have $2,238,000—a huge $1,000,000 "lost."

The rate of return you achieve on your investments, therefore, is critical to your wealth, and it's important to be very particular about this element, especially when it comes to how much you pay for your investments. We'll look at this in more detail later on, so for now just understand why even the smallest difference makes a huge impact.

Yes, believe it or not, compounding needs money to work its magic, and money is the basic ingredient that time and the rate of return spice up! How much money you choose to invest and put into your Wealth Cooking will make a significant difference to the time it takes you to achieve financial freedom.

Back to our example of $250 invested each month: if you decide you want to speed things up and put just $10 more into your wealth pot each month, at retirement you'd have $3,360,000. That's a huge $330,000 gained for just $10 more a month and only $6,000 extra in total!

Before we continue, let's talk a little bit about money. More money means having the support you want and doing what you want, when you want, with whom you want, and all without having to ask permission from anyone. No bosses, no deadlines, no performance appraisals—in other words, being in charge of your own life. Since this is so obvious . . . why are we even talking about it?

 Well, because sometimes, the obvious is so obvious that we miss the point! When we talk about wanting to be wealthy, what are we really talking about: money, or the things we believe money will give us?

There's a pretty big difference between the two! Does having more money mean having more freedom, security, fun, peace of mind, or whatever else it is you believe it will bring you? Not necessarily.

Being financially rich certainly provides material convenience, but we all know plenty of rich people out there who are completely miserable. Sometimes they miss the whole point of being wealthy.

One of the greatest lessons I learned on my journey to financial freedom was that money was not the be—all and end-all!

"Hold on a second, Ann!" you might be thinking. "If money isn't the point of all this, then what are we talking about?"

You see, money isn't the be-all and end-all, but it is an incredible and very powerful resource that you absolutely must master in order to live the life you desire.

The key points here are Mastering Money and Living the Life You Desire. And to do this, you need to know exactly what it is you really want. You see, what we're really all looking for is the feeling that we associate with being wealthy. The house we want can give us a sense of comfort. The car we desire can heighten a feeling of importance. Travel and toys can bring excitement and stave off boredom. The passive cash flow can give us freedom to choose not to work.

But you don't have to wait to have massive amounts of money in order to have all of these things or to experience the feelings of being proud and excited about your life.

The goal isn't to become rich in order to be free. In fact, it's the other way round. Choose freedom now and understand that you have all the freedom in the world already in your life—freedom of choice. Ironically, when I fully understood this, my financial wealth expanded exponentially.

I'd finally understood that Wealth = Money + Rich Life Experiences.

So how do you become wealthy now? Financially speaking, you do this by mastering the recipes of wealth and realizing that every decision you make is your choice. Every dollar and cent you spend is your choice, and what you get for it in return will create either money heaven or hell.

You ensure that some of your spending decisions result in your buying and creating passive Income streams, which will gather momentum over a few years, expanding, as compounding does its job, and then continuing to do so with other passive Income structures. This way, you receive material wealth.

You also ensure that you get massive value from your other spending decisions, ensuring that your money brings you rich life experiences now—not some time down the road when you're "rich." This is easy if you really know what it is you want, what emotion it is that you're after. So spend some time discovering what it is you really want to feel and choose to have that in your life *Now!*

TIPS

- While you're brushing your teeth before you go to bed, tonight and every night while you build your financial freedom, ask yourself the following four questions:

  - What am I proud of in my life right now, in relation to my wealth and my money?

  - What am I excited about in my life right now, in relation to my wealth and my money?

  - What am I committed to in my life right now, in relation to my wealth and my money?

  - What am I grateful for in my life right now, in relation to my wealth and my money?

- Now here's the deal: you can't stop brushing until you have at least one answer in each category! Look on the bright side. Either you're going to finish building your wealth foundation with the most amazingly sparkling clean teeth you've ever had or you're going to discover so many things that you're really proud of, excited about, and grateful for in your life. Hopefully, it will be both!

- Please answer the questions fully and also be aware of how you feel when you get your answers. If nothing clear pops up in your mind, just keep asking the same question until something does.

- I also encourage you to put these answers down in your journal.

This is about mastering your focus, you see—so, please make sure you do it! Remember, you've made a commitment to play full-out—after all, what have you got to lose? The worst thing that could happen would be for you to stay where you are, but the best would be to see you well on your way to financial freedom!

5.

Your Wealth Cooking Scales

You've discovered the Wealth Flow patterns and learned about the Four Wealth Flavors and the drawers in your Wealth Pantry where each flavor is stored. Now you're going to be rolling up your sleeves and getting your Wealth Kitchen set up for success.

Having the right tools to work with makes all the difference. In Wealth Cooking, there are five essential tools. Without them, you'll be severely limited in your Wealth Cooking, not to mention frustrated!

It's crucial to understand Wealth Flows, Flavors, Ingredients, and Spices. These fundamentals are vital to the success of your Wealth Cooking. They enable money to stay and grow in your life. Knowing the differences, as well as the relationships, between an Asset and a Liability, As well as Income and Expenses, allows you to successfully "read" the money flow in everything and to differentiate between, say, a money-sucking Liability and a wealth creating Asset. The first two Wealth Cooking tools—the Wealth Scales—are all about helping you to "read" the money flow.

The Wealth Scales

You'll need two Wealth Cooking Scales. The first scale (your Income Statement) measures the movement and activity of your money in present time, while the second scale (your Balance Sheet) measures the cumulative impact of all your money activity in the past.

You need these tools to see clearly how money is flowing in your life and whether the flow is moving you closer toward your Wealth Feast or in the opposite direction. The scales also allow you to see what changes need to be made in order to enjoy a healthy, wealthy flow—the healthiest, wealthiest flow possible. A flow that will take you to financial freedom!

Before we get to look at the exact results your current money flows have created in your life—so that you'll be able to determine exactly what you need to do to be financially free—you'll need to roll your sleeves up and actually work out where you are right now.

This is where the scales come in: the Income Statement measures the quick flow of money in your daily life (the ins and the outs), whereas the Balance Sheet reflects the result of all the ins and the outs over time (say, your financial life to date). If the Income is the river, then the Balance Sheet is the canyon carved by the river.

The Wealth Scales will become your favorite and most important tools in your Wealth Kitchen. They may seem tedious at first, and it may take a while to get them sorted, but once you have set them up, you just need to keep them updated—and this, you'll see, will get easier and easier.

Well, time to roll up your sleeves and put on your Wealth Chef apron. Let's get your first set of Wealth Cooking tools sorted out!

I realize that for some of you this may seem as enjoyable as having your teeth pulled. I also know that you may be tempted to skip this step. If you don't feel like doing this, then it's exactly why you must!

Here are some exercises for you: as you feel resistance, write down in your Wealth Journal your thoughts on what's coming up for you. These thoughts and the words in your head will give you some great clues as to your beliefs about money. Perhaps you don't want to see your own profit or loss in cold hard numbers, but remember: this exercise isn't about your self-worth—it's about your Net Worth!

In any case, you need to know where you stand and exactly what you have to start off with, if you are to create your Wealth Feast.

(If you skip this part, by the way, you're just confirming that you are, at best, an Octopus Money Cook, which you'll learn all about in Chapter 9!)

A preliminary piece of advice: avoid the tendency to try to make the numbers look better than they really are. This is your tool and your wealth measuring scale.

If you try to skew the numbers, the only person you'll be fooling will be yourself. Remember: nobody else needs to see these, so please don't overvalue your Assets, and be completely honest about your current spending!

Let's start with your Income Statement.

Income and Expenses

To begin with, you'll create an annual Income Statement reflecting your money flows for the past year. An annual Income Statement is also a good way to start, as it will pick up some of the annual or quarterly payments we all have.

TO RECAP

- Your Income Statement is a snapshot of your current Income and Expenses. This is the dynamic, fluid part of your Wealth Pantry, with regular flows of cash in and out.

To help you with this, you can download a sample Income Statement spreadsheet from The Wealth Chef website (see the link at the end of the book).

The example Income Statement shown is the first one that I created when Dave and I got married and we decided to get our joint Wealth Kitchen really organized.

Start with the Income part of the statement by adding up all the sources of Income in your life. These include your pretax monthly employment Income (if you have

	Income			Expenditure	
- ANNIE'S INCOME STATEMENT -					
INFLOWS			**OUTFLOWS**		
	Monthly	Annually		Monthly	Annually
Income 1 — Annie's Salary	$3,400	$40,800	**INVESTMENTS**		
Income 2 — Dave's Salary	4,200	50,400	Pay Yourself First	190	$2,280
			Pension	395	4,740
			Subtotal: Investment	585	7,020
Investment Property Net Income	640	7,680			
Dividends from Shares	0	0	Save to Spend	580	6,960
Royalties from My Books	120	1,440			
Passive Business Income	0	0	**TAX**		
Other Income: Bonuses, Gifts, etc.	400	4,800	Tax: % of Income	33%	33%
			Tax Amount	2,891	34,690
			FIXED SPEND		
			Insurance — Home, Car, Medical	280	3,360
			Insurance — Life, Disability & Critical Illness	120	1,440
			Utilities — Water, electricity, Gas	185	2,220
			Domestic Help, Child Care	230	2,760
			Bank Fees	25	300
			Satellite / Cable TV	85	1,020
			Mortgage / Rent	1,400	16,800
			Consumer Debt Payments	540	6,480
			Subtotal: Fixed Spend	2,865	34,380
			VARIABLE SPEND		
			Telephone — Cell, Fixed Line	175	2,100
			Food	450	5,400
			Entertainment	210	2,520
			Transport / Gas	160	1,920
			Exercise & Personal Care	120	1,440
			Vacations	190	2,280
			Clothing	250	3,000
			Pet Food, Veterinarian	75	900
			Gifts	90	1,080
			Cash — Miscellaneous	300	3,600
			Home Maintenance	140	1,680
			Car Maintenance	80	960
Total Pretax Income	8,760		**Subtotal: Variable Spend**	2,240	26,880
Post-tax Income	5,869	70,430	**Total Expenditure (Outflow)**	8,581	102,970
Profit or Loss INCOME - EXPENDITURE=	179	2,150			

your own business, this is the salary you pay yourself), Income from investment property, Income from passive businesses, Income from royalties, interest from bank accounts, dividends from equity, child maintenance support, child benefits (if you're lucky enough to live in a country that provides these), and pension or annuity income. Basically, all and any money that flows in.

What we're aiming for here is to establish an accurate record of your average monthly and annual income. Although the spreadsheet that you can download is set up to input a monthly amount and then calculate the annual number, you may find it easier (particularly if you have irregular or uneven Income flows) to look at last year's Income and simply divide it by 12.

Our aim is to be as realistic as possible, so please do not overestimate year-end bonuses or inheritances that you think you may get! It would be better to leave these out of your Income Statement for now, and if they do arrive, then you'll have a great additional sum to put straight into your Asset Drawer!

Now, your Expenses. Take a deep breath, get out a big flashlight, and shine that light in the dark scary place that most people either don't want to look in or try to kid themselves about.

Let's start with last month's bank account statement. I recommend you get your last three months' bank statements out and use these to start listing your Expenses. Most banks have online banking where you can download these in a format to pull straight onto a spreadsheet. This is exactly what I do. You're aiming to create an accurate picture of how money has been flowing in your life up to this point, not what you would like to believe has been happening, and the more actual information you have, the more accurate your wealth measures will be.

I have a spreadsheet called "Spending" and every month I download my hubby Dave's and my monthly expenses from our bank accounts and put them onto that spreadsheet.

I like to keep it simple, with just four columns:

1. The date

2. The vendor with whom I incurred the Expenditure

3. The amount

4. The category

You'll need to put your Expenses into spending categories (dividing up your spending into similar types of Expenses) in order to make them easier to work with. I recommend you create 10 to 15 different spending categories, such as: food, entertainment, car maintenance, pets, insurance, utilities, bank fees, personal care (hair and cosmetics), sports and gym subscriptions, hobbies, magazines, and so on. It's important to allocate a category to each and every expense.

Create enough categories to be able to differentiate spending patterns, but not so many that you can't see the wood for the trees!

- SPENDING -			
Date	Vendor	Amount	Category
May 1st	ABC Shoes	$160	Ann's Fun Pot
May 2nd	Yummy Foods	215	Food
May 3rd	Bushy Investments	210	Wealth Pot
May 4th	Zeb's Insurance	122	Insurance
May 5th	Well's Pharmacy	105	Personal Care
May 6th	Movie Magic	43	Entertainment
May 7th	ABC Cooking	72	Food

A spreadsheet is the simplest way to do this. Be specific. Don't just put: Credit Card X, $2,000! Itemize each expense on your credit card statement, add each one to the spending record, and then allocate them a spending category.

The Income Statement shown above lists some category examples, but please feel free to create your own. The point about categories is that they enable you to list your Expenses in manageable pieces. When there are too many lines and individual portions, we can't see the patterns—and, as you now know, patterns are really important when it comes to creating wealth!

Remember to include any direct debits/standing orders you have that go straight from your bank account, or which are deducted directly from your salary. These will include: pension contributions, medical aid or insurance contributions, investment contributions, insurance premiums, subscriptions, and so on.

Also, remember to add any lump sum Expenses you pay annually that are not on your last three months' bank statements. Divide these by 12, in order to get a monthly amount.

A final category of Expenses is loan repayments: put in the monthly repayment amounts for each and every loan you have.

Once you've put a spending category against each expense, you'll need to sort the monthly spending by category, so that you get a total per category. This will be the amount that you'll then transfer to the expense column of your Income Statement.

And let's not forget Income tax! Remember, in the Income portion of your Income Statement we added up your pretax earnings. So include the tax you pay in your Expenses. After all, for most people, this will be one of their biggest Expenses.

You'll notice I also have a category called Investments in the expense section of my Income Statement. This is because these are also outflows, in terms of money flowing in my life, but these outflows flow into my Asset Drawer and not out of my life.

Now, add up all your Expenses to arrive at the current total of your Expense Drawer.

Take your time!

Take the time to do all this properly. You're setting up your Wealth Cooking kitchen and the time spent now to get your Wealth Kitchen tools in great shape will reap benefits for the rest of your life. So, as painful as it may feel now, do it right and you'll be thankful you did!

Ask yourself: what can I do to make this fun? Put music on that makes you feel great. If snacks work for you, put your favorites in bowls all around, so you can reach out and grab a supporting handful whenever you feel like bolting.

When you first do this, you may find that your Expenses total is much smaller than your Income total. Before you start celebrating and rush out to spend the difference, don't get too excited! Although the surplus may look real on paper, the money is gone if it isn't in your bank account.

If you're not yet tracking your Expenses, you may find that you have many cash withdrawals and no idea where that money went!

So, for now, just add a cash row to your expense sheet and put the "extra" amount in there. But try hard to identify those sneaky missing Expenses and estimate where the cash has been spent! These are the rats in your Wealth Pantry that gnaw away at your wealth. As you start tracking your Expenses and get better at managing your money, your goal will be for every cent to be accounted for.

If you can't account for less than 10 percent of your Expenses at the moment, you're doing relatively well and have a fairly accurate analysis of where your money is going. Even so, you'll want to get the miscellaneous amount down to less than 5 percent of your spending.

If you can't account for more than 10 percent of your Expenses, then you'll need to implement a detailed spending tracking system for a few months in order to create awareness in this area. This is, essentially, a spending diary where you write down everything you spend money on, every day, for one month minimum.

TIPS

- Buy a small notebook and each time you spend on anything, whether in cash or by debit or credit card, quickly jot down the date, the vendor, the spend category, and the amount. At the end of every day, add up the spending by category and at the end of every week, add up the categories from each day.

- By the end of the month, you'll have a very accurate picture of your spending in each of the categories you identified and you'll be able to fill in those gaps on your Income Statement!

- It's vital to track your spending as you go along. Don't worry about keeping loads of receipts in bags and carting them around with you until the end of the month! This is just irritating and painful, and most people won't spend the time needed to then sort out all the receipts, transfer the information to a tracking system, and see what's going on!

- The key to successful Wealth Cooking and an effective Wealth Kitchen is to keep things simple: every tool you have must be easy to use, otherwise you won't use it— it's as simple as that!

So now you have all your inflows on the Income side and your outflows on the Expense side. It's time for the big reveal! Deduct your Expenses from your Income and record the difference. This number tells you immediately if you are creating or consuming wealth.

If the number is negative, you're spending more than you earn and you now have your first big clue as to where you need to focus more energy.

If the number is positive, well done! You're making a profit in your life and you've mastered the first principle of wealth: spending less than you earn.

The Balance Sheet

Now, after having successively created your first Wealth Cooking tool, it's time for the Balance Sheet. You are about to discover exactly how far along the road you are in creating your Wealth Feast!

To help you with this, you can download a sample Balance Sheet spreadsheet from the Wealth Chef website (see the link at the end of the book).

Let's start with your Assets: add up all the things you currently own that can, and should, add money to your pocket, remembering the definition of a Wealth Asset: something that can put money into your pocket.

These will include: the current value of your pension plan (both your personal and company pensions, if this is the case); the current market value of your home, as well as of any Income-generating investment property that you own; the value of any equity investment portfolios you have, be they shares or mutual funds; any positive cash balances you have in bank or savings accounts; the current market value of any business that you own (that is, what you'd get for it if you were to sell it now, less any business loans you may have); and finally, the market value of any intellectual property you directly own, such as online products, books, films, and other things that you earn royalties on. (This is a bit harder to estimate, but as a rule of thumb, take 60 percent of your annual Income from these products and use that as a rough estimate for now.)

Add the Assets together and you'll arrive at the total of your Asset Drawer.

Please note, we are not including any cars that you own, furniture, jewelry, or the like, as these are not Income-generating Assets! They are, in fact, objects that sit in what author Robert Kiyosaki calls the doodad pile. These are the things you choose to have, but that have no role in your wealth creation. Other doodads include clothes, your music system, the holiday you

- BALANCE SHEET -			
ASSETS	**Value**	**LIABILITIES**	**Amount Owed**
Investment Properties	$195,000	Investment Property Mortgages	$162,000
Annie's Pension	18,000	Credit Card Debt	2,800
Dave's Pension	28,000	Student Loans	24,000
Equity Investments	8,000	Overdrafts	6,500
Business	0	Car Loans	11,350
Other	0	Store Cards	0
Principal Private Residence—Home	205,000	Home Mortgage	172,000
TOTAL	454,000	**TOTAL**	378,650
Wealth-generating Assets: all those above, excluding the home you live in	249,000	Liabilities, excluding the home you live in	206,650
FINANCIAL FREEDOM NET WORTH (Wealth Assets - Liabilities = WEALTH POT)	42,350		

went on, and your flat-screen TV—it's all just stuff! For the purposes of your Wealth Cooking, all these belongings are nice to own but have absolutely no Wealth Cooking value.

To calculate the wealth-generating Assets, we'll also need to deduct the value of your current home, if you own it. You're doing this because, although your home has real value (unlike most doodads), it isn't an Income-generating Asset as long as you're living in it and so it doesn't form part of your Wealth Feast. And we're only interested in Assets that contribute to your Wealth Feast!

Now that you've completed the Assets part of your Balance Sheet, let's fill in the Liabilities: add up all the things you owe.

Add your mortgage on your home, mortgages on investment property, any car loans you may have, student loans, credit card debt, debt owed on store cards, and any other loans and debts. Although you've excluded your car and your home as Wealth Cooking Assets, you must include any loans you have against these in your Liabilities drawer.

Then add up all your Liabilities to arrive at the total of your Liability Drawer. Don't panic if your Liability Drawer is fuller than your Asset Drawer. That's why we're here—to do something about it!

And so, what's your current Net Worth?

(Note: you might want to sit down when you get to this part!)

Deduct the total of all your Liabilities from the total of all your Assets. This will show you your gross Net Worth. This is nice to know, but we want more. We want to know your wealth-generating Net Worth—that is, the size of the pot that will feed you and support you when you're financially free.

Remember, you're financially free when you have a pot of Assets that can generate enough Income to cover your living Expenses.

To calculate your wealth-generating Net Worth, subtract the value of your home from the total of your Assets and subtract your home mortgage from the total of your Liabilities. Now subtract your Liabilities, less your home mortgage, from your wealth-generating Assets and you have your current wealth-generating Net Worth.

This also tells you the exact size of your current Wealth Feast Pot. Remember—your wealth-generating Net Worth is the amount of money you have that can be put to work for you.

If you're looking at your total wealth-generating Net Worth and see a negative number, keep breathing! It will be negative (more Liabilities than Assets) for 95 percent of the population.

The problem is that this picture never changes for most people, until they either stop working and sell their home or cash in part of their pension. Their house may be full of the latest gadgets, and they may drive fancy cars and wear the latest designer clothes, but in reality, they're broke. If you fall into this category, however, don't despair! Just the simple fact that you're reading this book (and doing the exercises!) and actually know where you are financially puts you in with the tiny, but significant, minority of financially savvy folk! You're taking action, and that means you're well on your way to changing things in your life.

By the time you've mastered all The Wealth Chef recipes and created all five Wealth Cooking tools, you'll know how to reduce your Expenditure, increase your investment contributions, and get yourself out of debt—and so you will be well on your way to financial freedom.

6.

The Obsession Magnet & the Big Why Sieve

You've now created your first two Wealth Cooking tools—congratulations!

In doing so, you had everything pertaining to your money in front of you. I'm sure that the very fact of getting it out of the closet and moving it away from the places where it was creating long dark shadows in your life made you realize it wasn't so scary after all.

Okay—perhaps it was a little scary! Perhaps you discovered that your Wealth Pantry is just a little unbalanced. Maybe your Liability Drawer is almost full. But now you know—and clarity brings you power: now you can take the blinders off and actually do something about it!

With your personal Income Statement and Balance Sheet completed, you now know whether you're currently making a profit or incurring a loss in your life and are also aware of the results of your past money actions, which have created your current Net Worth. With these tools in your Wealth Kitchen, you'll be able to see very quickly which areas you need to focus on and where you need to make changes.

Now you're going to create the next set of Wealth Cooking tools: the Obsession Magnet and the Big Why Sieve.

While the Income Statement and the Balance Sheet show you what's happening to your money now and the result of your actions in the past, the magnet and the sieve take you into the future: they shape how you cook and what you'll be cooking in your Wealth Kitchen.

The Obsession Magnet is the tool that pulls you forward. Your Obsession Magnet gives you focus and direction. It's your vision, the Financial Freedom Vision, the vision you're creating now.

The Big Why Sieve is your reason for it all. Your Big Why Sieve serves two primary purposes. First, it's a powerful filter through which you make money decisions. Decisions on how you direct the flow of your money and what you spend it on, ensuring that your money decisions take you closer to your Financial Freedom Vision and the life you really want to experience. Second, your Big Why Sieve gives you your reason to stay on the path you have chosen.

Your Big Why is about knowing, deep inside of you, why you absolutely must achieve this Financial Freedom and what precisely you'll be able to do, have, and create by having achieved it.

Stop: this is important!

Achieving financial freedom is only 20 percent about the techniques and is 80 percent about the person.

Designing your Financial Freedom Vision and describing it in writing is all about the person. It's about having the discipline to plan first, rather than just driving off with no idea where you're going or what you want. This is possibly the most important step in creating your Wealth Feast. It's the founding step, which is where your motivation comes from. And it will serve you as a compass too, as you embark on your wealth journey.

Expect great things. If you do, they will happen!

Anytime you believe something with certainty, conviction, and power, it will manifest itself in your life—bring it to life, as it were. This is the difference between hope and certainty. Most people are "negative manifesters." They believe they won't find love, won't be rich, won't be successful—and so they're not. You are the creator of your world. If you believe that you can do something, then you're right. If you believe you can't, then you're also right.

Motive really does matter, and the magnet and the sieve are all about this. The purpose of goals is not just about the end point. Goals are also about who you need to become in order to achieve them and what the journey will bring you. Goals help us focus on what we want: they direct our energy toward achieving it. Energy flows where focus goes.

So, please: set yourself some powerful, awesome, scary, hairy, audacious, and, above all, exciting financial freedom goals!

There is an oft-quoted story about a Harvard University research project into the power of written goals. It goes something like this: scientists polled a class in 1953 at Harvard and found that 3 percent of students had written their financial goals down; in the class reunion of 1973, they found that 97 percent of the people who'd written their goals down had achieved them, compared to only 34 percent of those who hadn't.

I also know, from personal experience, that writing a goal down makes a significant impact on the probability of my achieving that goal. For example, when I finally decided to set very specific financial goals in my life, my wealth skyrocketed!

The act of writing triggers a whole bunch of neurons in the brain that aren't activated by just thinking about something. Writing is also the first act of bringing something out of your mind and into this world. It triggers the reticular activating system (RAS), a network of nerves in the brain that control our states of awareness and attention. This system functions as a filter or doorway that either accepts or rejects the overwhelming stimuli, which wc all cncounter while we're awake.

What the RAS accepts or rejects and allows into our consciousness depends on what we've told it to be important to us. You set this "filter" by consciously choosing to think about certain things. One of the most familiar examples is when you buy a new car and suddenly start seeing the same make, model, and color all over the place!

They were really there all the time, but your RAS only "allowed" the information to enter your conscious mind once you told it that that particular piece of information was important to you—because you set your RAS to look for that make, color, and style of car.

When you write down what you want in your life, you effectively set your RAS, that is what makes you start noticing opportunities that will bring you closer toward your goal.

In a nutshell: writing it down is the first step toward achieving the goal!

The second reason for writing down goals is something called the Ebbinghaus Effect. Hermann Ebbinghaus was a German psychologist, the first to investigate the properties of human memory.

He studied why we remember certain things and discovered two key reasons: primacy and immediacy. He found out that within seven days of learning something new, if a person hasn't written something down or reviewed the material, she'll lose 50 percent of the knowledge gained. Wait another seven days, and she'll lose 50 percent of the 50 percent, and so forth.

And within six weeks, she'll remember little to nothing!

This is why it's important that you repeat, practice, and saturate yourself with what you're learning, until it forms part of you. Otherwise, like a bungee cord, you'll lose the stretch and go back almost to where you started.

If you don't write your goals down and review them regularly, then guess what? You're going to forget them! The reality is this: with the pressures of day-to-day life, most people either forget about or give up on their goals.

Writing a goal down is also an act of commitment, a commitment to you, a commitment to be and to have all in your life. So you need to create and maintain a compelling future that will pull you forward toward it (your financial freedom goal).

Maybe you feel this part is a bit "out there" and you'd rather stick with just the technical parts of this money business. Well, I've been there and done that and yes, you may achieve some financial success—but I can tell you this: as you come across challenges and barriers on your way to creating your financial freedom, it's your Big Why that will keep you going.

If you have no idea why you want to achieve financial freedom, your fuel and focus will quickly dissipate. You need to make your Why so big that when you hit a speed bump, you'll still be able to see it way above the hump, calling you and reminding you, "You can get over this hump, too!"

I meet a lot of people who really want to make a difference in the world, who want to contribute and help. Being African, I'm also intimately aware of the impacts and effects of poverty. Now, here's the thing: if you want to help the poor, don't be one of them! Be the change you want to see in the world first. (Mahatma Gandhi said that.)

The tools I'm talking about will be a key part of ensuring you are that change!

Your obsession magnet– a strong, powerful, and clear vision

You're now about to create your Financial Freedom Vision: a strong, powerful, and clear vision to aim for. This is the life of your dreams, if you only dared to write it down! The life where you're living your purpose and leading the life you're meant to lead.

What you focus on ultimately becomes your reality, so make this vision huge! The more vivid you make your vision, the more certain you'll feel about it happening in your life.

Any time you believe something with absolute certainty, conviction, and power, you bring it to life. Clarity of vision is vital—it makes the difference between hope and certainty.

As I mentioned before, the majority of people are "negative manifesters": they believe they won't find love, won't be rich, won't be successful—and so, they're not. But you are the creator of your world, so there's absolutely no reason not to create the world you want!

And the key to this is to describe your financial vision with as much clarity as possible and in great detail. You'll find it easier and much more effective if you can get someone to help you with this, someone to keep asking you the questions (see below), but you can also do it yourself. No worries!

First, find a place where you won't be disturbed, put on some great music that makes you smile, and have your journal in hand. You're about to describe your ideal, financially free life in great detail. You're going to describe it using every sense and fiber of your being. (You should see it, feel it, hear it, touch it, and even smell it!)

Before you start writing, though, let your mind warm up to the idea. For some of you, it may have been a while since you let your imagination go wild, so don't rush it.

Just imagine if money were never a problem again . . .

If you could have it all:
- Who would you be?
- What would you have?
- What would you do?
- What would you contribute?

Imagine you had unlimited wealth, all the money you could ever dream of and more . . . In this place of deep fantasy, really imagine everything and anything you would do, be, have, and contribute if money were unlimited. Let your mind flow freely through a sea of ideas.

Breathe it all in and experience what it feels like to have the freedom to achieve, have, be, and do anything you dream of when you're financially free. When you have all the money you need to live the life of your dreams.

Close your eyes and let your imagination go wild . . .

Now, start describing your financial vision, using all of your senses to do so.

What do you see?

Describe everything you see, as if you were there right now, in the minutest of details: from your dream home, garden, car, yacht, playthings to all the people and places who are there with you in your vision.

How many rooms are there in your home? What's in the garden? Where are you traveling to? How do you travel? What do you do once you're there? Where's your home, which country . . . how many homes do you have, in fact?

Go wild, the more you *see*, the more you get! Who is there, and what are they doing? What sort of "work" do you do? How are you spending your time? What's the legacy that you're creating?

What do you hear?

For example, if you imagined children running toward you, then what would they be shouting or saying? How do you answer them? Or if you are driving that red Ferrari, describe the noise it makes and what people are saying. Is the stereo system on? What music is playing? Are there sounds of nature? If so, which sounds? What else can you *hear*?

What do you feel?

When you see yourself in your dream home and hear all the sounds you hear, what do you *feel*? In your car, do you feel the leather beneath you, the seat and the throbbing of the engine?

As you run your hands over the things around you, what do they feel like?

Do you feel great inside with that special person next to you? Or if children are running toward you, screaming in delight, and you scoop them up, what and how do you *feel*?

When you're flowing in your "work," how does that make you feel? When you're contributing and making a difference by doing what you love doing, how does that make you feel? When you see what you have created, what do you feel?

Remember, this is *your* vision. Make it big, make it exciting! Go for it! Feel it!

What do you smell and taste?

Smell is the most primordial and evocative of our senses.

What can you *smell* in your vision? Is there a specific smell of the earth or the ocean where you choose to live and play, now that you have all the money you need to live your life fully? A scent of the people there with you in your vision—a perfume or aftershave, for example?

And what can you *taste* as you're seeing, hearing, feeling, and smelling all these things?

What can you afford to eat? Is there a taste to your environment? Notice all these details and write them down.

TIPS

- Once you've created your Financial Freedom Vision—your Obsession Magnet—you may want to keep a vision board that you can fill with images and words that describe it. Or you can add images to your Wealth Journal.

- Keep adding layers to your vision as things come to you, making your vision richer all the time. Make this so enticing that you simply can't stop creating it!!

- You can also record your own Financial Freedom Vision and listen to it when you're traveling or just as you go to sleep. Put on some great music that feeds your imagination, press Record, close your eyes, and describe your financially free life in infinite detail, loving it, seeing it, feeling it, living it, now!

- Keep your Financial Freedom Vision alive by stepping into it each and every morning when you wake up. Take a few moments to bring this picture into your mind. Make it powerful and really feel yourself in it. See it in your life, feel it in your body, and hear the sounds. Keep turning the volume up every day.

- Go big and make the feast of your life a masterpiece!

Your Big Why

The Big Why is the most important driver and the primary reason why you either will or won't successfully achieve financial freedom in your life.

As you come across challenges and barriers on your journey to becoming a Wealth Chef—which you will—it will be your Big Why that will keep you going. If you have no idea why you want to create your feast, then you will soon lose your focus and your fuel will quickly run out.

You need to make your Why so big that when you hit a large speed bump, you'll still be able to see your financial freedom goal, way above the hump, calling you and reminding you that, yes, you can get over this hurdle, too.

So, please take your Wealth Journal and write down the essence of your Financial Freedom Feast, the primary purpose for creating it, and the ultimate reason why you're committed to it. Find a phrase that captures this and put it at the top of the page—something that encapsulates the vision you've created. Use words that feel right for you, but make sure you write it in the first person and in the present tense!

For example:

- "I am financially free," *not* "I want to be financially free."

- "I am living my life purpose with all the money I need supporting me."

- "I have an abundance of money in my life, and I'm living life on my own terms," *not* "One day there will be an abundance of money."

- "Money flows to me easily, and I always have all I need to be and do, and I have everything I wish," *not* "Money will flow to me easily."

- Now, here comes the most important part: under your vision phrase on top of the page, write down why you absolutely must achieve this.

Answer these questions fully. Ask them out loud and then quickly write down everything that comes to you. For example:

- What will achieving your financial freedom give you?

- What will achieving it enable you to do, be, have, and create?

- What will achieving it mean to the people you love?

- What will it enable these people to do, be, have, and create in their lives?

- Who will you become in the process?

- What kind of person will it take to achieve all that you want? (Describe the character traits, beliefs, values, and virtues that this person embodies.)

Awesome!

Now, on a new page, write down what not achieving this goal will cost you in your life.

Answer these questions fully. Again, ask them out loud:

- What will not achieving your financial freedom cost you in your lifetime?

- What will not achieving it cost the people who you love?

- What won't you be able to do, have, be, and create if you don't achieve financial freedom?

Now, use your imagination. Go forward five years and imagine you haven't made any progress toward your financial freedom. Picture where you are and what you're doing.

- What does that feel like?

- What have these lost five years cost you?

- How about 10 years?

- What can't you do, be, have, achieve, create, or experience because you haven't achieved financial freedom or made any progress toward it?

- What will the people you love not be able to do, be, have, or create because you haven't moved forward?

- What kind of person will you become if you don't achieve your financial freedom?

Perhaps this is making you feel uncomfortable?

Good. This should feel tough. After all, this is what it will feel like if you don't change where you're headed. This is what it feels like to not achieve your financial freedom.

Really allow yourself to go there and experience what it feels like to not achieve this in your lifetime. Understand what it feels like to never have enough money to live the life you know you could or to live up to your potential—to never have the money you need to live your purpose or shine your light fully.

If you're not feeling uncomfortable by now, then you need to go deeper and be really honest with yourself. You see, comfortable is the worst you can be if you want to make real change, because feeling uncomfortable makes us take action—and action changes our results.

You should be feeling a strong push and pull inside you now, pushing you and pulling you toward your financial freedom. You should feel a sense of urgency to take action. If not, go back to your Big Why and do the exercises all over again!

Well done!

You've done it! You've successfully created the next two tools in your Wealth Kitchen. You know what your Wealth Feast is all about, and you know what it looks like, feels like, sounds like, smells like—even what it tastes like. And you're getting hungry.

You know your Big Why, you know why you absolutely must create this Financial Freedom Feast, and you know what you'll be able to do, achieve, have, and create once you have it in your life. You also know with certainty what *not* creating your Financial Freedom Feast would cost you and those you love. And you don't want to go there!

Keep adding to your Obsession Magnet and your Big Why Sieve. You'll soon see very clearly how you'll be using them, when we get to the Core Recipes. They help you stay committed and make better daily wealth decisions, decisions that take you toward your feast and not away from it.

Think about the last vacation you planned: did you look at brochures with wonderful vivid photos, get information about your destination on the Internet, talk about all the things that you would do once you arrived, and get all excited about it? I'm sure you also identified all the things you needed to do in order to make your vacation happen: tickets that needed to be booked, finding your visa and passports, clothing to be packed, arranging your leave from work, organizing house-sitters to feed your dog, and so on.

All of these were the smaller steps to making your vacation happen. Having a clear vision of the holiday you wanted— knowing what you wanted out of it, your *why*, and identifying all the steps you needed to take to get there—helped you focus and gave you a clear set of actions to take.

Everything we do, we do to meet a need or a value that we hold as important. Goals help us focus on what we want, and they direct our energy toward achieving what we want—which, as we know, is all about experiencing a specific emotion.

Albert Einstein once said, "I am enough of an artist to draw freely upon my imagination. Imagination is more important than knowledge, for knowledge is limited, while imagination embraces the entire world."

Use this powerful resource within you and turn your dreams into reality, starting now!

Turning your dream into reality really does begin now, with equipping your Wealth Kitchen with the tools it needs!

And remember, simply doing the best you can is never good enough. You must do whatever it takes. You must keep making the decision to create financial freedom over and over again, and these two tools—your Obsession Magnet and your Big Why Sieve—will help you make that decision.

7.

The Wealth Health Certificate

Can you prove that you know what you're doing and can be trusted with money?

Believe it or not, there is a "certificate" that tells the world exactly that! And this certificate is exactly why there's some truth to the old adage that the rich get the best deals (meaning, actually, that the people who understand money get the best deals). A key part to understanding money is having a great Wealth Health Certificate.

The Wealth Health Certificate is the fifth tool you need in your Wealth Kitchen and the last one you'll need before you start cooking: I'm talking about your credit score.

Your aim is nothing short of having the best credit score in the class! Just imagine being the person to whom the banks offer the lowest interest rates on borrowing, the cheapest car insurance, and the best financing deals. This will soon be you, because Wealth Chefs know how to create and keep their score high.

Know your status

We're talking here about your credit status and, more specifically, your credit score. The better your credit score, the less interest you have to pay, and now that you understand compounding, you'll know that even 0.5 percent in interest, over time, makes a huge difference.

You may recognize the term "credit score" but perhaps have no real idea exactly what it is and what it means to you. Well, whether you know it or not, just about every bill you pay is tracked by the two main credit bureaus: TransUnion and Experian. They each have a big file on you! In it, they keep information on whether you pay your bills on time, how much debt you have, who you hang out with, and also how good they are with their credit!

All this information is then thrown into a huge financial food-mixer and then out the other end pops your personal credit score. The score is based on a risk measure invented by a company (Fair Isaac) and is called the FICO credit score.

The FICO score is a numerical number that lets companies know how good or bad a credit risk you are. It ranges from 300 (you're very bad) to 850 (you're a credit angel). All credit bureaus use this scoring method as a basis and then just tweak it a little, according to their own system.

When you apply for a credit card, a loan, or a phone contract, the relevant company will take a look at your credit score to see how responsible you are with your debt. Landlords also use credit scores to see if you'll be a reliable tenant. Even insurance premiums can be influenced by this score.

If you've got a great score—in other words, you're really good at paying on time and haven't extended yourself to use all your available credit and also don't apply for credit too often—then they'll most probably be delighted to do business with you and offer you a good deal. The better the score, the more companies will want to help you (it's in their interest!), offering you sweet deals. This means lower interest rates on your mortgages, car loans, and credit cards.

The bottom line is, you want to know your status. Wealth Chefs know their score and keep it updated. In almost every country now, you're entitled to get your credit score from each credit agency, once a year, for free—so, use it!

Six easy steps

There are six easy steps to getting your credit score and keeping it healthy.

1. **See what everyone's saying about you**: Google TransUnion and Experian and get your score now. In most countries, you'll be able to see it almost immediately online.

2. **Fix the typos.** Given that your credit record spans nearly a decade of your borrowing activity, it's

no surprise that errors sometimes occur. Some common credit-reporting blunders include: out-of-date addresses, closed accounts being shown as open, and downright false information.

3. **Mend your uncreditworthy ways, ASAP!** Those self-inflicted credit wounds (such as a history of late payments, defaults, and generally bad credit behavior) will fade from your record over time. You won't be able to wipe out accurate information from your credit report (nor can any firm who offers to do so for a fee, no matter what story they spin, by the way!).

4. **Since your most recent behavior carries more weight than old news**, vow that from this day forward you're going to be a financial Goody Two-Shoes! This means paying your bills on time, every time, and keeping your debt level low, compared to the credit available.

5. **Memorize this mantra: it's plastic, not cash.** A credit card is just that, a credit card. Even though you've been deemed worthy by some entity to borrow $50,000 doesn't mean you actually have $50,000, nor that you now need to go and spend $50,000!

6. **Ignore bankers' rules on what is an "acceptable" level of debt.** Your debt-to-Income ratio is the measure of how much debt you carry to how much money (after taxes) you have coming in.

In the world of lending, it's accceptable to carry 25 percent of your Income in debt. You should only ever use this ratio for good debt. (You're only going to consider good debt, once you've proved yourself to be a great Wealth Chef by eliminating all your bad debt!)

Rinse and repeat. You can see that fancy maneuvers are not what you need to keep your credit looking spiffy and your Wealth Health in tip-top shape. Just keep your spending under control, pay your bills on time, don't apply for extra credit too often—and, then, don't be shocked when you find yourself among those with elite credit-score status!

So, there you have it!

You now have five powerful Wealth Cooking tools ready to help you create a juicy Wealth Feast!

8.

Planning the Feast

Congratulations! You now have your Wealth Kitchen set up with your Wealth Tools. You have your personal Income Statement and Balance Sheet and you know your Net Worth. With these in your Wealth Kitchen, you'll be able to very quickly see which areas you need to focus on and where you need to make changes.

Now we're going to get into your Financial Freedom Feast Vision: exactly what financial freedom means for you, the specific financial result you're after, and the Net Worth you need in order to achieve that—so that you're finally financially free! We'll then break that down into very achievable (less scary) bite-size chunks.

A smart Financial Freedom Feast Vision should be specific, measurable, achievable, realistic, and time-based. So let's make yours very *smart*!

How big a feast
do you want it to be?

The number one reason why most people flounder around in the dark and don't get what they want, financially, is because they don't know what they want, specifically.

When I ask people what they'd like in relation to wealth, they usually say something along the lines of the following: "Lots of money" or "Enough money so I don't have to work again."

When I press them and ask, "How much is a lot of money?" or "How much do you need to never have to work again?" most people stare at me blankly and make a wild guess: "$1 million," "$2 million," "$20 million?" When I push them even further and ask, "Why $1 million, $2 million, or $20 million?" they're unable to say.

At this point, they usually turn the question back to me: "Ann," they ask, "how much money do I need to be financially free?"

My answer's always the same: "I haven't got a clue!"

I am not being deliberately obtuse here! You see, the amount of money required to be financially free is unique for each and every person, as unique as we all are as individuals.

People also sometimes ask me how much money I have, believing that this must be the magic target, since I'm financially free. But how much money I have, or how much anyone else has, is completely irrelevant to you. The only thing that matters is how much money you have and how much money you need in order to be financially free.

What does financial freedom mean for you, and how will you know when you get there? Less than 5 percent of the world's population knows the following: you're financially free when you have a large enough pot of Assets that earn money for you and provide you with the Income you need, without your having to work. (And if you do work, it will be from choice, not necessity!)

The simple objective of the Financial Freedom Wealth Recipes is to fill your Wealth Pots full of Assets, so that you earn sufficient passive Income to support the lifestyle you desire. You'll be financially free when the Assets in your Wealth Pots can create passive Income that exceeds your Expenses. In other words (in a language that you now understand): when your Net Worth—your Assets minus your Liabilities—is big enough to give you an Income that exceeds your Expenses. It is as simple as that.

Now, let's make sure you are very, very clear about what exactly it is that you want.

Let's get specific!

For this, you'll need three of the Wealth Tools you created and a calculator. You'll need your juicy Financial Freedom Vision, your Income Statement, and your Balance Sheet. (If you haven't created them yet, do so now: you can't move forward without them!)

Just how big your Wealth Pantry needs to be depends on your Expenses. More specifically, it's determined by the Expenses you choose to have in order to live a certain lifestyle. Looking at your Income Statement, write down the total amount of your current Expenses. This is what it costs you to live your current lifestyle.

Now, add to that an additional amount of money that you believe you need to live the lifestyle you desire. This is the lifestyle you described in your Financial Freedom Vision. Perhaps it's the same lifestyle you have now, just without having to work. Or maybe you want a lifestyle twice as big, and, therefore, twice as expensive as your current lifestyle.

Go with your gut; trust what it's telling you, as, in any case, you can always increase or reduce the amount. And remember, it's your choice! The lower your Expenses, the easier and quicker it will be to create financial freedom. But also: life is to be lived and loved—so go for it! It's all possible.

Now add this amount to your current Expenses.

Next, go to the Income Projector Table at the end of this chapter. Find the monthly Income closest to the one that you need to lead your desired lifestyle, and see the Net Worth you require for that Income.

We're using a rate of return or interest rate of 8 percent to calculate the Net Worth you need to produce an Income to cover the Expenses you've identified (if you choose to stop earning an Income actively). Although you'll be achieving returns exceeding 12 percent to 5 percent on your Assets, we'll use 8 percent to take into account inflation and tax as well to give us a buffer. (I prefer to underpromise and overachieve in all aspects of my life.)

The Net Worth Number you've identified may be somewhat shocking at first. If you suddenly feel a bit weak at the knees at the size of the number, breathe deeply! It is easier to achieve than you may think. (Don't worry about the "how" just yet; that's what the five core recipes are all about!)

This is also a great opportunity for you to become aware of some of your issues around money. What thoughts popped into your head when you saw the number? What emotions swept through your body? Notice these things, and write them down in your Wealth Journal—they're really important, as they give you clues as to your beliefs about money and wealth.

Wow, so now you know exactly what you're aiming for! The Net Worth Number you've just identified is the exact size of the Wealth Pot you need in order to be financially free. This is the size of your total Financial Freedom Feast.

It's awesome knowing the end result you're aiming for, but it can sometimes seem overwhelming—so let's do this bit by bit.

Let's carve your Financial Freedom Feast up into manageable courses (easier to cook, easier to digest).

The seven courses

Print out the Financial Freedom Feast Menu and the Menu Planner from the Wealth Chef website (see the link at the end of the book) or make a copy of the ones at the end of this chapter.

You're about to create your own Financial Freedom Feast Menu. You know how big the whole feast needs to be, so now you're going to define what exactly you need in each course that will add up to your total Financial Freedom Feast. (Not only will this give you total clarity in terms of the whole feast, but you'll be able to focus on creating one course at a time.)

There are seven courses in your Financial Freedom Feast. As each course is described below, fill in the monthly Income you need to achieve that course. Once the monthly Income for each course has been determined, you'll calculate the Net Worth needed for each course, using the Income projector once again. The first course you'll be creating is . . .

- Course 1 -
Absolute Zero

This is more of an *amuse-bouche* than an actual Wealth Feast course. And just like an *amuse-bouche*, this first tasty morsel on the Freedom Feast Menu serves to get you excited about the Financial Freedom Feast, by offering a glimpse of the feast to come.

Absolute Zero is created when you achieve zero. Yes, you read that correctly! You've achieved Absolute Zero when your Net Worth is zero—which is either when your Assets are as large as your Liabilities or when you've destroyed all your debt and have no Assets or Liabilities. If you fail to aim for it (because, like so many people, you're busy focusing on Income and the big dream), you'll never get past it.

Absolute Zero is the magical doorway between negative Net Worth and positive Net worth. It's the ultimate taster that stimulates your wealth palate and gets you ready for your Wealth Feast.

When you finish cooking this course and achieve Absolute Zero, give yourself a huge congratulatory hug! Most adults in the Western world don't reach this place for a long, long time—if ever.

- **Assets—Liabilities = 0**

- Course 2 -
Protection Pâté

A cash safety net blended with protection insurances: this is your first Wealth Dish and your first course in positive Net Worth territory. The purpose of Protection Pâté is to provide you with a safety net that lets you swing a bit higher, breathe a little easier, sleep more soundly, and generally know you'll be taken care of in the event of a fall.

A cash safety net is: enough liquid Assets (basically cash) to cover your basic living Expenses (food and shelter) for a minimum of two to nine months, depending on your own comfort zone. This should be readily accessible in a facility such as an interest-bearing account or money market fund.

Insurances: a term life insurance policy (when you die, your family or those you provide for will be taken care of financially) and a critical illness/disability insurance (to protect you and your family in the event of your becoming sick or disabled and unable to earn an Income).

- **Cash Safety Net** = Monthly Basic Living Costs x Feel-safe Months = ... Lump Sum

- Basic Living Costs = Shelter + Food

- Course 3 -
Security Soup

To cook your Security Soup Course, you need to have a large enough Net Worth to provide you with Income to cover your secure living needs.

Secure living includes:

- Shelter costs—rent or mortgage repayment
- Food
- Utilities—electricity, gas, water
- Transport

- Insurances—car, house, life, disability
- Taxes and rates—property, not Income tax
- **Security Soup** = Secure Living Costs
  = ... monthly Income

- Course 4 -
Vital Veggies

You have to eat your greens! Vital Veggies get cooked when your Net Worth is large enough to provide you with an Income for secure living costs (same as above) plus the following:

- Children's education

- Basic entertainment (this should be about 50 percent of what you're enjoying now)

- Clothes and reasonable luxury items (these should be 20 percent of what you think your ultimate luxury spending will cost you)

- **Vital Veggies** = ... monthly Income

- Course 5 -
Rat Race Roast

You get to eat Rat Race Roast when you can choose whether to work or not.

This is the Freedom Feast Course where you cover your current Expenses and is often described as financial independence, because you can be independent of active work.

The dish is made out of exactly what you're living off now, minus any amount that you're currently putting into investments.

This is a seriously sexy Wealth Dish. When you get to cook it, you are out of the rat race forever! Some of you may decide that this is the perfect end to your wealth journey, and for those of you that do, I say: celebrate! Most people *never* get here, even when they retire.

- **Rat Race Roast** = ... monthly Income

- Course 6 -
Freedom Flambé

You've reached the dessert course. Freedom Flambé is reached with the financial freedom Income you calculated earlier. It's the Income you need to live the lifestyle you desire, the lifestyle you described in your Financial Freedom Vision. This is where you get to add all your toys, charities, fantastic trips, deluxe pamperings, private chefs, and all the other things you dream of.

- **Financial Freedom Flambé** = Rat Race Roast Income + the additional Income you need to cover the lifestyle you want = ... monthly Income

- Course 7 -
Absolute Abundance

There is an extra course: Absolute Abundance. This course isn't for everyone and to create it requires serious focus, commitment, and determination—but it's magical!

Absolute Abundance comes when you've accumulated a Net Worth that provides you with sufficient Income to do virtually whatever you want to do, whenever, wherever, with whomever you want to do it, and as often as you want!

Imagine some of the things you'd like to do, and add these to your Financial Freedom Flambé Income. An example of the increased monthly Expenditure would be: the cook you now employ to make all your meals, the personal trainer who keeps you in great shape, the monthly membership to the country club or the annual three months' world traveling.

A lot of people get serious stage fright here. So ban any "How would I do this?" or "Do I deserve it?" thoughts and loosen any tight clothing, because you need to let rip, go wild, and *dream big!*

You may prefer to come back to this part later. For now, just add some estimates of the Income you think you'll need to support this Ultimate Dream life. Have fun and go onto the Web to research the prices of custom-made Lear jets, a gorgeous catamaran in the Caribbean, or a private game reserve off Kruger Park.

What charity will you establish and how much do you need for this? Dream big, bigger, and even bigger still! If you can imagine it, you can create it. All you need are the right skills, mind-set, and a huge vision!

Now add this all up and add it to your Financial Freedom Flambé Income.

- **Absolute Abundance** = ... monthly Income

Your financial freedom goal is getting smarter

You should now have a list of monthly Income amounts needed for each of the seven Freedom Feast courses:

1. Absolute Zero   = ...0.......... Net Worth

2. Protection Pâté   = ... Lump Sum

3. Security Soup   = ... Monthly Income

4. Vital Veggies   = ... Monthly Income

5. Rat Race Roast   = ... Monthly Income

6. Financial Freedom Flambé = ... Monthly Income

7. Absolute Abundance   = ... Monthly Income

Transfer these Incomes to the table on your Financial Feast Menu Planner. Go back to the Net Worth—Income Projector Table and write down the Net Worth required to produce each Income Level on your Financial Freedom Feast Menu.

- MONTHLY INCOME PROJECTION FROM NET WORTH @ 8% INTEREST RATE -

NET WORTH	INCOME	NET WORTH	INCOME	NET WORTH	INCOME	NET WORTH	INCOME	NET WORTH	INCOME
$0	$0	$2,500k	$16,667	$4,950k	$33,000	$7,400k	$49,333	$9,850k	$65,667
100k	667	2,550k	17,000	5,000k	33,333	7,450k	49,667	9,900k	66,000
150k	1,000	2,600k	17,333	5,050k	33,667	7,500k	50,000	9,950k	66,333
200k	1,333	2,650k	17,667	5,100k	34,000	7,550k	50,333	10,000k	66,667
250k	1,667	2,700k	18,000	5,150k	34,333	7,600k	50,667	10,050k	67,000
300k	2,000	2,750k	18,333	5,200k	34,667	7,650k	51,000	10,100k	67,333
350k	2,333	2,800k	18,667	5,250k	35,000	7,700k	51,333	10,150k	67,667
400k	2,667	2,850k	19,000	5,300k	35,333	7,750k	51,667	10,200k	68,000
450k	3,000	2,900k	19,333	5,350k	35,667	7,800k	52,000	10,250k	68,333
500k	3,333	2,950k	19,667	5,400k	36,000	7,850k	52,333	10,300k	68,667
550k	3,667	3,000k	20,000	5,450k	36,333	7,900k	52,667	10,350k	69,000
600k	4,000	3,050k	20,333	5,500k	36,667	7,950k	53,000	10,400k	69,333
650k	4,333	3,100k	20,667	5,550k	37,000	8,000k	53,333	10,450k	69,667
700k	4,667	3,150k	21,000	5,600k	37,333	8,050k	53,667	10,500k	70,000
750k	5,000	3,200k	21,333	5,650k	37,667	8,100k	54,000	10,550k	70,333
800k	5,333	3,250k	21,667	5,700k	38,000	8,150k	54,333	10,600k	70,667
850k	5,667	3,300k	22,000	5,750k	38,333	8,200k	54,667	10,650k	71,000
900k	6,000	3,350k	22,333	5,800k	38,667	8,250k	55,000	10,700k	71,333
950k	6,333	3,400k	22,667	5,850k	39,000	8,300k	55,333	10,750k	71,667
1,000k	6,667	3,450k	23,000	5,900k	39,333	8,350k	55,667	10,800k	72,000
1,050k	7,000	3,500k	23,333	5,950k	39,667	8,400k	56,000	10,850k	72,333
1,100k	7,333	3,550k	23,667	6,000k	40,000	8,450k	56,333	10,900k	72,667
1,150k	7,667	3,600k	24,000	6,050k	40,333	8,500k	56,667	10,950k	73,000
1,200k	8,000	3,650k	24,333	6,100k	40,667	8,550k	57,000	11,000k	73,333
1,250k	8,333	3,700k	24,667	6,150k	41,000	8,600k	57,333	11,050k	73,667
1,300k	8,667	3,750k	25,000	6,200k	41,333	8,650k	57,667	11,100k	74,000
1,350k	9,000	3,800k	25,333	6,250k	41,667	8,700k	58,000	11,150k	74,333
1,400k	9,333	3,850k	25,667	6,300k	42,000	8,750k	58,333	11,200k	74,667
1,450k	9,667	3,900k	26,000	6,350k	42,333	8,800k	58,667	11,250k	75,000
1,500k	10,000	3,950k	26,333	6,400k	42,667	8,850k	59,000	11,300k	75,333
1,550k	10,333	4,000k	26,667	6,450k	43,000	8,900k	59,333	11,350k	75,667
1,600k	10,667	4,050k	27,000	6,500k	43,333	8,950k	59,667	11,400k	76,000
1,650k	11,000	4,100k	27,333	6,550k	43,667	9,000k	60,000	11,450k	76,333
1,700k	11,333	4,150k	27,667	6,600k	44,000	9,050k	60,333	11,500k	76,667
1,750k	11,667	4,200k	28,000	6,650k	44,333	9,100k	60,667	11,550k	77,000
1,800k	12,000	4,250k	28,333	6,700k	44,667	9,150k	61,000	11,600k	77,333
1,850k	12,333	4,300k	28,667	6,750k	45,000	9,200k	61,333	11,650k	77,667
1,900k	12,667	4,350k	29,000	6,800k	45,333	9,250k	61,667	11,700k	78,000
1,950k	13,000	4,400k	29,333	6,850k	45,667	9,300k	62,000	11,750k	78,333
2,000k	13,333	4,450k	29,667	6,900k	46,000	9,350k	62,333	11,800k	78,667
2,050k	13,667	4,500k	30,000	6,950k	46,333	9,400k	62,667	11,850k	79,000
2,100k	14,000	4,550k	30,333	7,000k	46,667	9,450k	63,000	11,900k	79,333
2,150k	14,333	4,600k	30,667	7,050k	47,000	9,500k	63,333	11,950k	79,667
2,200k	14,667	4,650k	31,000	7,100k	47,333	9,550k	63,667	12,000k	80,000
2,250k	15,000	4,700k	31,333	7,150k	47,667	9,600k	64,000	12,050k	80,333
2,300k	15,333	4,750k	31,667	7,200k	48,000	9,650k	64,333	12,100k	80,667
2,350k	15,667	4,800k	32,000	7,250k	48,333	9,700k	64,667	12,150k	81,000
2,400k	16,000	4,850k	32,333	7,300k	48,667	9,750k	65,000	12,200k	81,333
2,450k	16,333	4,900k	32,667	7,350k	49,000	9,800k	65,333	12,250k	81,667

Le Menu

- *Amuse-bouche* -

Absolute Zero   Net Worth = 0

- *Entrée* -

Protection Pâté   Lump Sum =

- *Soupe* -

Security Soup   Net Worth =

- *Salade* -

Vital Veggies   Net Worth =

- *Plat Principal* -

Rat Race Roast   Net Worth =

- *Dessert* -

Freedom Flambé   Net Worth =

- *Digestif* -

Absolute Abundance   Net Worth =

Your financial freedom goal is getting smarter by the minute.

You've made your Financial Freedom Feast very specific: you can measure it, it's achievable (especially broken down into step-by-step courses to create), it's realistic, because it's based on your own lifestyle and vision, and now we need to make it time-based.

Decide how quickly you want your feast made. It doesn't matter how long it takes you to create it. What matters is that you do.

Remember, very few people ever get to achieve true financial freedom. So if it takes you until you're 55, 65, or 75, so what? You'll have achieved a financial feast for when it really counts. And if you do it quicker, fantastic. Against each Financial Freedom Feast course, add the year by which you'll have created the required Net Worth for that course.

Remember: Absolute Abundance isn't for everyone; you may choose to aim for Freedom Flambé or you may decide Rat Race Roast is just great for you. If so, add your target years up to the course you intend to create. It's your feast and your life, so design it to work for you. It also doesn't matter how long you take to get there or which route you choose: all that matters is that you arrive.

Now look at your Balance Sheet and mark on the Menu where you are already. You may be surprised. Perhaps you've already achieved one or more courses. If so, celebrate and put a big smiley face in the target year for those courses you've already achieved!

My goal is that every person reading *The Wealth Chef* achieves at least Rat Race Roast. I believe that not only is this totally achievable, but also totally inevitable if you:

- Master and implement the five Wealth Chef Recipes.

- Keep focused on your Wealth Feast Vision and why you're creating it.

- Resist any temptation to rob yourself along the way.

- Get the teaching and support you need, and make it all as automatic as possible.

Whether you choose to create the last two courses (Financial Freedom Flambé or Absolute Abundance) is a very personal choice that depends entirely on your values and also on "What blows your skirt up," as my nephew Bruce would say!

You can also accelerate your feast by taking actions in all four drawers of your Wealth Pantry (your Income, Expenses, Assets, and Liabilities).

You do this spending less, investing more, paying off your bad debt, making your money work harder, and by expanding yourself so you can bring in even more.

You can achieve each course even faster by simplifying your life and reducing your Expenses. This is actually the greatest "get rich quick scheme" and the only one that works! Simplifying all aspects of your life not only significantly reduces your Expenses, by making your Financial Freedom Feast even easier to create, but it also triggers all sorts of wealth magic, adding value, time, and space into your life—but more of that later!

Remember, it's all about choice. The faster you plan to create your feast and the bigger the feast is, the more skills, support, and mentors you'll require as a Wealth Chef.

That's it! You have your Financial Freedom Feast quantified, planned, and made seriously smart. It feels good, doesn't it?

TIPS

- Put your menu in your journal or somewhere you'll look at it often. Keep looking at it and experience how great it feels to be in control of each step of your journey. This is what you need to be focusing on.

- And if you ever get to a point where you say "Why the hell am I doing all this?" come back to this chapter and also read your Big Why!

9.

Meet the Chef

The chef who's going to create your Freedom Feast is you. You are the only person who can create your wealth . . . so you need to know the kind of Wealth Chef you need to be to make it happen!

Most people believe they are just who they are, and that this can't change. As you will discover, this isn't so. Although our identifier (who we believe we are) is one of our strongest drivers, we can change it—and our behavior—as a result. One of the best ways of doing this is by having powerful, hairy, scary, and audacious goals like the ones you've already set for yourself. The reason we have big goals in life is less about the goal itself, and more about who we need to become in order to achieve the goal.

In fact, you've already begun this change just by reading this book, completing the exercises, and taking action. You're already upgrading your Wealth Cooking skills and are well on your way to becoming a Wealth Chef!

Just as we did with your Wealth Flow patterns, the first step in any change is to know where you are right now and where you want to go. In Chapter 3 you learned about the different Wealth Flow patterns of different Money Cook types. If you didn't do so at the time, go back and determine what type of Money Cook you used to be and what Wealth Flow pattern you used to create with your money.

Self-awareness is key. The more we can recognize our behavior patterns and the ensuing results, the quicker we can change the ones that aren't helping us achieve our goals. And to do this, we need to know the behavior patterns that are necessary to achieve our goal—and so, you now need to learn the characteristics and behaviors of a successful Wealth Chef.

You may have noticed I have used the terms "Money Cooks" and "Wealth Chefs."

Cooks prepare food. There is no guarantee that what they produce will be edible and nurturing or that they're at all able to create a feast. The same applies to Money Cooks. They may deal with money, but there's no guarantee they know how to create wealth with it.

As you discovered when you learned about the Money Cook types, the characteristics of each type have nothing to do with the amount of Income earned, but everything to do with what the different Money Cook types do with that Income and the Wealth Flow patterns they create as a result.

A chef, however, is a highly skilled professional who is proficient in all aspects of food and who creates quality feasts. Wealth Chefs not only deal with money, but they also understand the ingredients of wealth: they know how to work with money, how to make it, keep it, and grow it, so that it works hard for them.

What it takes to be a Wealth Chef

Once you've mastered and embodied the characteristics of a Wealth Chef, your financial freedom is assured.

Wealth Chefs are clearly aware of the need to invest and divert money into their Asset Drawers. However, unlike TV Dinner Money Cooks, they're actively involved in their investment decisions and work hard to give their money the best possible environment to grow in.

Wealth Chefs understand that they are the creators of their own life and take responsibility for everything in it. They practice the daily disciplines and skills of the Wealth Chef. They have a clear, written-down Financial Feast Vision, and they know precisely why they will and must create it in their lives.

They also know from their Wealth Measuring Tools exactly where they are now, and what size their Financial Freedom Feast needs to be. They have a Financial Freedom Feast Menu that details the steps to get them there, as well as the ingredients for each course, so that achieving their Feast is completely viable.

They also constantly use the five core Wealth Recipes to create their Financial Freedom Feast courses and ensure that their Net Worth is growing.

Their approach is: keep it simple.

Wealth Chefs consciously choose their own lifestyle and get massive value for every bit of money they allow to flow out. They choose a lifestyle that enables them to enjoy life and at the same time keep their Expenses well below their Income. Wealth Chefs are not concerned with what "everybody else" or what the "cool people" are doing. They are prepared to do things differently and live differently, and to do it now, so that they can do things and live differently later on.

Wealth Chefs eliminate all consumer debt from their lives and at the same time invest in things they understand, such as straightforward stock market trackers, which provide the opportunity for realistic returns over the long term, as well as in solid investment properties, which return a positive cash flow from day one.

Wealth Chefs make financial freedom their priority and pay themselves first, by ensuring money flows into their Asset Drawer first. They then simply look for Assets with a good Wealth Flow—one that brings money into their lives—and set up automatic investment plans to keep on buying those Assets. They don't get fancy. They buy good stocks, trackers, exchange traded funds (ETFs), or mutual funds and hold out for the long term. They understand the power of money invested over time. This is the power of compounding—the Wealth

Yeast—you're already familiar with, but you'll get to love it once you start using it in your Wealth Cooking.

Wealth Chefs constantly look out for successful Wealth Chefs they can model themselves on (such as Warren Buffet—to my mind, the most successful Wealth Chef ever), and study them to learn their unique know-how.

Wealth Chefs also read books such as *The Millionaire Next Door,* by Thomas Stanley and William Danko, to discover for themselves who the real financially free people are and what they actually do with their money.

Wealth Chefs have decided to be financially free. This may sound weird, but actually making this decision and sticking with it is a key characteristic of a successful Wealth Chef.

As you know, I'm a civil engineer and I've spent over 20 years working around the world on amazing infrastructure projects. The thing that always struck me during these years was how much of the budget and effort that went into these projects was always taken by those invisible pieces of the structure, usually underground. This was to ensure that the visible pieces—"the pretty bits"—stayed up and lasted! And to do that, you need to go down really deep and create strong foundations, so it doesn't all come tumbling down when the wind blows.

I was watching a program on the world's tallest man-made structures recently. The tallest was the Buji Khalifa in Dubai, standing at an impressive 2,722 feet tall (829.8m). The second tallest was the Petronas Towers in Kuala Lumpur, at 1,483 feet (451.9m). What really fascinated me, though, was the depth of the foundations, the depth needed to allow the buildings to rise so high. In the Petronas Towers, the foundations go down a staggering 532 feet (162m)—so a third of the height of what we see of this incredible building is repeated below ground, and it had to be built first.

One of the reasons people don't become financially free is that they can't be bothered to dig down and put the solid roots in place before they build their mansion. They want the fancy awnings and glitzy aboveground stuff that everyone can see—and so they become the Borrow More Money Cook. But it's all smoke and mirrors, floating on hooks in the sky, and as soon as a gust of wind blows—as it always does—it all blows away, and they're left standing naked in the storm again, bewailing their fate.

Wealth Chefs understand, respect, and love their foundations, and they have the discipline to dig down as deep as necessary, long before they have a big tower for the world to see.

Wealth Chefs are focused, disciplined, committed, and determined, and they believe in the power of their dreams. They know the value of the tower they're raising and so are prepared to do whatever it takes to make it solid and strong.

Likewise, if you do the work and implement the recipes in your life, you too will have a financial foundation that can stand whatever life throws at you. It will withstand the earthquakes and the storms that will come, but because you'll have dug down deep, you'll be able to relax, knowing that your wealth can not only support you, but that it can also see you through the night.

As you embark on your financial freedom journey and commit to becoming an awesome Wealth Chef, I need to warn you about one type of Money Cook you haven't met yet: the Octopus Money Cook.

The Octopus Money Cook

The Octopus Money Cook is intelligent and really, really, really wants to become financially free. The problem is that, unlike Wealth Chefs, octopuses have no discipline or focus. It's as if they were on roller skates: lots of frenetic activity, but going absolutely nowhere. I know, because I used to be one myself!

Octopus Money Cooks realize that they need to invest and buy Assets, but they want to make investing exciting. They also want money really fast and so fall into the "get rich quick" trap. They are essentially gamblers who haven't yet understood how money actually works. They're endlessly looking for the "Wealth Secret" (a miracle ingredient) and new and exciting get-rich-quick schemes, even though their Wealth Scales reflect their lack of success.

Financial Freedom, however, is about a Wealth Feast for life, not a quick sugar binge!

People tend to overestimate what they can achieve in a year and significantly underestimate what they can achieve in ten years if they just keep building on the foundations that they've created. The problem is that so many people just experience the same year, ten times over!

The Octopuses' impatience and need for instant happiness make them walk away from the foundations they're creating time and time again, off in pursuit of the next business, investment, opportunity, or job. The following is what their financial foundations typically look like.

Octopus Money Cooks start the work; they're all fired up and start digging down. But soon, they become impatient and think, "This isn't working. It's going too slowly," and so they abandon this attempt and start building a new tower, using a new technique. After the initial flurry of excitement, they discover that it's going too slowly again, so over and over, they start from scratch. And at the end of ten years they have piles of incomplete towers, all lying and useless.

If they'd just stuck with the one tower, however, dug down deep first and built a solid foundation, they'd have been on top of the world by now, and it would have gotten easier and easier, as well as faster and faster. It would be completed. That is what a Wealth Chef does.

If you're a bit of an adrenaline junkie, if you like a bit of chaos and thrill, that's great—just don't try and meet that need from your Wealth Cooking!

So, where are we?

Now, not only do you have your own Wealth Cooking Tools in your Wealth Kitchen, but you've also defined very clearly what financial freedom means to you, you know the amount of Assets you need in your Wealth Pots in order to achieve it, and you also know the manageable Financial Freedom Courses you need to create.

(Perhaps you've even discovered that you're further along than you thought you were!)

You've also discovered what type of Money Cook you used to be, why you got the wealth results you used to get, and what type of Wealth Chef you need to commit yourself to becoming in order to cook the feast you've designed!

10.

Wealth Recipe #1: Easy Wealth Pie

What's your Financial Freedom Feast Menu looking like? How is it feeling, sounding, and smelling? I hope you really went there and let your inner child have a field day, adding all the things you'll do, be, have, create, and experience with your financial freedom—uncensored and abundant! Keep going back to it and adding to it. I do, the whole time! I always joke that the more I travel, the more I learn, the more things I experience, the longer my dream list gets, and the bigger my Freedom Feast becomes!

We're now going to get down to the core Wealth Recipes you must learn, master, and practice over and over and over again, until you achieve your Financial Freedom!

Wealth Recipe #1 is Easy Wealth Pie. To support your pie-making and pie-carving, you're going to fine-tune your carving skills and learn how to squeeze the juice. You're going to discover just where the mice have been eating away at your Wealth Pantry and learn how to plug those holes, so that you have less flowing out of your Expenses Drawer, while maintaining the same quality of life—in fact, maybe even better. And you'll also discover how to use the amazing Wealth Cooking tool you've already created, your Big Why Sieve.

So, with no further ado, let's dive straight into Wealth Recipe #1—where you learn how to keep some of what you make!

In this recipe, we're going to use the most fundamental Wealth Cooking technique.

Pay yourself first

Some of you might say, "I already know this!"—to which I reply: "If you're not using it, then you don't know it!"

Obviously, you are in control of what you spend. You get to determine what your lifestyle costs you. It's your choice as to what type of car you drive or whether you have one at all, what kind of house you live in and where, whether you eat out five times a week or once a month, whether you have your nails done weekly, or weather you have the latest cell phone. You're in control of all those decisions. We all get bombarded every minute of the day by others telling us what we need, who we need to be, what our kids need if we really love them . . . the list goes on and on, but at the end of it all, you are the one who decides.

I'll be sharing with you how to make this easier, but first, you need to take responsibility for your financial situation and know that it is your choice.

You've already learned that wealth has very little to do with Income. You've realized that while most people stare at their Income Statement, it's actually the Balance Sheet that holds the wealth, and financially free people know that it is there where they have to focus.

For me, true wealth is a healthy balance of Net Worth and joyous flow. To create sustainable true wealth, you need to balance the respect and value of money with the joy and abundance it can bring us. We need to nurture our wealth by giving it the fertile environment it needs to grow and, at the same time, allow it to breathe. Like energy, it needs to flow and move to stay fresh and alive. If you squirrel it away, hanging on to it tightly, fearful of losing it, it can never grow nor work for you and bring you the very things you want from it. Likewise, if you squander it, ignore it, or use it inappropriately, it won't be able to support you in achieving your vision either.

And so, for me, true wealth is a vital and delicate balance of structure and flow.

Conscious spending is the key. All you need to do is have your eyes wide open and be conscious about the choices you make every second, every minute, and every hour of your day, because it's the decisions that we make each and every moment that shape our destiny. Make sure your decisions are taking you toward the life of your dreams and not away from it. Because if you don't give money the structure it needs to flourish and grow, it will wither and wander off to someone else!

The structure that money needs is provided by solid money management.

I always say to people, "Show me how you manage your money, and I'll tell you how close you are to financial freedom." Most people don't want anything to do with management, because they believe it restricts them. Words like "budget" make them suffocate. Now, here's the secret: good money management actually creates freedom!

You are about to get to know a system, inspired by T. Harv Eker, that is set up to change your life forever. This isn't a budget—this is your Spending Plan, so please feel the difference already. The Spending Plan is easy, simple, and effective.

The first point is to keep it simple, because if we overcomplicate things, then we won't use them. So let's start sharpening our knives and learn how to carve the Wealth Pie.

- Recipe #1 -
Easy Wealth Pie

Recipe #1 is as follows: when Income comes into your Wealth Kitchen, immediately carve it up into six portions, putting each portion into a different pot. Each pot will have a unique and important purpose.

When we're talking about Income here, we mean net Income after tax. If you don't pay withholding tax or the equivalent taken out of a paycheck, then you need to add a seventh pot for the tax man. Now, put a big smile on that pot because paying taxes is what I call a quality problem! Whatever your tax rate is, take that amount out first and put it into pot number seven, and then simply divide the rest up into the following percentages:

- Pot 1 -
Your Investment Pot

Ten percent of every piece of Income you get goes into this pot. This money is only to be invested. *You never spend this money.*

The purpose of this pot is to create a lump sum that will feed you in the future in the form of interest and dividends. You'll invest this in stocks and shares or bonds and property but you can never, ever spend it! Allow it to grow big and fat. You pay yourself—your freedom—first. Please don't stress right now about where to invest. We'll get to that in Wealth Recipe #2.

One of the things I always get asked here is, "Shouldn't I put all this money into clearing my debts first?" My answer is no; what we're doing here is creating new wealthy habits first and foremost. You must create the habit of investing—and while you're doing that, you pay off debt too. Energy flows where focus goes, and if you only focus on your debt, then that is all you'll ever know.

If you've developed a debt habit, like most of the Western world, we'll take care of that once and for all in Chapter 12. Part of breaking a habit is replacing it with a new one, and your new habit is going to be investing.

The great thing about investing is that you're still buying stuff—except now, you'll be buying things that feed you, not starve you! And if you don't do this, you won't be able to break your debt habit. Because, even if you do manage to clear all your debt, it's highly likely that you'll go straight back into it, if you haven't created a new investing habit.

- Pot 2 -
Your Save-to-Spend Pot

Ten percent of all your Income goes into this pot next. This is for long-term savings for spending, such as large Expenditures like a new car, a deposit on a house, your children's education, dream holidays, or weddings. You're going to save the money for those things now!

Save first, so when you come round to buying these things, you'll have the actual cash, instead of hoping you'll have the money and then being forced to use credit.

Here is where you'll also start building your cash safety net, if you don't yet have that in place. You determined how big a safety net that needs to be when you created your Financial Freedom Feast Menu.

- Pot 3 -
Your Growth Pot

I believe this is the most important pot in your Wealth Kitchen. It's the pot that finally changed my money story and my life forever.

This is the learning pot. I recommend that 10 percent of all you earn goes into your personal education. You need to expand the container called "you" to allow more to flow in. Just as the Asset Drawer is the only place where your wealth can grow and expand, so you are the only door through which money can enter your life.

Education allows you to learn how to create more money, how to keep it, and how to grow it faster. This pot allows you to have the mentors and teachers you need in your life to help you expand who you are and become who you need to be in order to have, keep, and grow more money in your life. This pot enables you to learn how to create success and expand it consistently.

We live in a world changing at phenomenal speed, where you need to be prepared by constantly learning. As Benjamin Franklin said, "If you think education's expensive, try ignorance!"

When it comes to money, my ignorance and my initial do -it-yourself attitude cost me a great deal of it, until I realized that I needed to spend money on my financial education. (I'll tell you more about my wealth story later on, but what I can say is that when I started investing in me, my wealth floodgates flew open—and stayed open!)

And so, I believe this is the best investment you'll ever make.

- Pot 4 -
Your Necessities Pot

This is your day-to-day spending pot. Fifty-five percent of your net Income goes into this pot. It's to pay bills, mortgage/rent, food, utilities, transport, insurance, and so on.

Now, if you're starting to feel a little queasy at the thought of "living on" 55 percent of your Income, that's good! Know this: it's the beginning of something new for you! If you're feeling like this, then ask yourself, "Just where have I been spending all that money?"

Most people can comfortably live on 55 percent of their Income. In fact, the majority of people who are financially free live within the 35 to 45 percent range. So, if you're not there yet and your day-to-day spending is more than 55 percent of what you earn, you need to discover two things:

- Exactly what you are spending your money on
- How to simplify your lifestyle in some way

You need to make some adjustments. Bring it down to 55 percent. This is your target. If it takes you a year to do so, that's fine—the point is to just do it! This is a long-term game we're playing here, and you simply have to spend less than you earn. It's one of the laws of nature!

Perhaps you're thinking that when you get a salary increase or make a few more sales, you'll be able to do it. Sadly, you won't. Please understand this: if you're spending more than 55 percent of what you earn on your necessities, this is a bad habit and you'll just keep spending the same proportion, irrespective of what you earn.

You must learn to carve now, no matter how small or large the amount is. You can try out all the get-rich-quick schemes (there's no shortage of them!), and you can double your Income (and you'll learn to do that, too), but if you consume all or more than you bring in, you will crash and burn. It's as simple as that, which is why this is Recipe #1!

- Pot 5 -
Your Fun Pot

Yeah—fun! And yes, you're actually allowed some of this! Seriously, having fun is vital for your financial well-being. Ten percent of every piece of Income you bring in goes to having fun.

Eating out, mini getaways, going to the movies, horseback riding, dancing, being creative, painting lessons, massages with hot stones—this pot is for those things that make you feel good and pampered—wealthy things.

But there is a rule with this pot: you have to spend all the money in it, if not monthly then at least every three months. You have to blow it!

This was a tough one for me, and sometimes still is. In the past, I created great saving and investing habits, but spending money on myself was seriously tough. In essence, I was suffering from *Wealth Anorexia*. Growing up during the height of the South African apartheid regime, I'd developed a number of really unhealthy wealth beliefs, attaching huge pain and guilt to having money—so much so that although I really wanted financial security, I hated spending money on me.

You must allow your free spirit some form of outlet. If you don't, it will burst out in some way or another, often causing a big mess as it does so, either in the form of binge spending or a huge money drama. And I kept having money dramas! Dramas that would wipe out my savings and investments—until I realized I was actually creating them, and that the root cause was my failure to allow myself to have fun and enjoy my money, guilt free.

You'll rebel against this key wealth recipe if you don't do this. You need to give your soul a creative outlet.

- Pot 6 -
Your Contributions Pot

Put at least 5 percent into this pot to donate to a charity or organization that you feel is creating a better world. If you want to turn it into 10 percent, then take the extra 5 percent from your Necessities. But remember, money isn't the only way to contribute. If you can't yet donate 5 percent, make time to contribute in other ways. That's it! Recipe #1: simple, but also immensely powerful.

So where do you actually put all this money?

Do you go and buy a big set of actual pots and split your money between each pot as it comes in and then have them and your money sitting around in your kitchen? Yes and no.

You need to have a minimum of two bank accounts: a transactional account, which you use for your everyday transactions, and an investment/savings account. Your Pot 1–Investment and Pot 2–Savings amounts need to be put into your investment/savings account as soon as Income comes into your life.

Your Necessities, Growth, Fun, and Contributions amounts can stay in the transactional account. When you update your Income Statement each month, track your actual spending in each of these categories against what your target spending is and adjust where necessary.

If banking is free or very low-cost where you live, you may choose to have more accounts, but remember, keep things simple!

I also recommend you have actual jars or pots in your home for "found" money and as a symbol of the great money manager you're becoming. Have fun decorating them and labeling them, and every time you find a few loose dollars or cents, put them into these pots in the Wealth Pie proportions.

Call them your Wealth/Freedom/Prosperity or Abundance Pots—whatever works for you! They'll serve to remind you that you're an excellent Wealth Chef and your money carving skills rock!

This is also a great activity for kids and a super way for you to teach them great money management skills early on in life.

Perhaps you're thinking, "But I have no money to manage"—*nooooo!!* Once you begin to manage it, you'll have plenty of it! Start managing your money as soon as you can. If you say you'll start once you've caught up, or when you get the next pay raise, so your Income is more than your Expenditure, and so on, it's a little like saying you'll start dieting and exercising once you've lost weight! The universe has a principle of management. You get more, once you show you can handle what you've already got. So start managing what you have now.

Managing your money is the ultimate get-rich scheme and the most lucrative thing you can do with your time and money right now.

I promised to teach you to find between 10 and 20 percent savings on your current spending without reducing your quality of life. To do this, you'll be using a new Wealth Cooking technique—juicing—and one of your coolest Wealth Cooking tools: your sieve.

Here we go!

Squeezing the juice

As a Wealth Chef, you need to squeeze the juice out of every cent you spend. You need to get value for your money, and most important, you need to spend less than you earn. You're probably thinking, "Yeah, right, Ann. Easy for you to say. I don't even have enough money for my month now, and you want me to spend less?" Yes, I do! Chances are, you *do* have some extra money, but it's leaking out of your Wealth Pantry and you haven't even noticed it. You'll need to be brutally honest about where your money is going.

Let's take a look at your Wealth Pantry again. The aim of your Wealth Cooking is to make your Income and Asset Drawers as big as possible, and your Liability and Expenses Drawers as small as possible, while living a quality life.

To do this, you have to reduce the cost of your day-to-day spending and increase your Income. Overspending is bizarre behavior and leads only to misery. We've created a break-even culture where most people believe that a successful month is one where the outflows match the inflows. You have to break out of break-even to create a Wealth Feast! Just focusing on increasing your Income won't do!

Ending the break-even habit is about achieving your target spend percentages. You can do so by increasing your Income while keeping your Expenses the same, by reducing your Expenses and keeping your Income the same, or—the best way—by increasing your Income and reducing your Expenses. For most people, reducing their Expenses is an easier place to start, rather than increasing their Income. We'll get back to increasing Income later. For now, we're going to slash your Expenses by squeezing out all the juice.

When you created your Income Statement, I'm sure you already discovered some items that you'd forgotten about. Or maybe you simply didn't realize just how much you were spending on certain categories. So first, work out how close you are to your spending targets and see in which categories you are out of balance. Start with the category where the gap between your target and actual Expenditure is the biggest.

You can decrease the gap between your target percentage and your current Expenditure percentage in two ways:

Set a percentage improvement target for each month—say, to decrease your gap by 2 percent a month over the next 12 months, or . . .

Challenge each item on your Expenditure list, with the aim of making reductions that will fill the gap.

When you're starting off, I recommend you do both. Challenging each item of your Expenditure really makes you question why you're spending that money and what it brings you. This helps increase your awareness of your spending habits.

When you start off challenging each item on your Expenditure list, your aim is to see where you can reduce your spending and so eliminate waste. Looking over your Expenses, you'll most probably notice a whole range of unconscious spending: things you've bought or money that's gone out without your even thinking about it—let alone getting value from it.

Another area of Expenditure that might surprise you is bank fees. These are nasty little amounts that add up quickly, like mice nibbling away in your Wealth Pantry. They can be significantly reduced by a little bit of research into different bank account options and by changing your bank.

Now, here's an amazing statistic: you are more likely to get divorced than to change your bank! So start being a demanding customer, value yourself and your money, and move to a bank and an account that makes *you* rich—not the bank! It's easy to change bank accounts, and most banks will do all the work around changing any debit orders you have. So no excuses: challenge each and every expense!

How you approach your expense slashing is going to make all the difference between success and failure. While you're going through your Expenditure, remember to keep your Wealth Feast Vision clearly in your mind. This is a treasure hunt. You're doing this because you value yourself. You're doing this because financial freedom and all the joy and happiness that comes with it are more important to you than some short-term sugar-rush fix brought on by spending all your money now.

Keep your Big Why
at the front of your mind

Keep your Big Why at the front of your mind and use that awesome tool, your imagination, to see how each reduction in your spending is helping to create your Wealth Feast. I do this all the time. Seeing where I can reduce my Expenditure is a game I play. Yes, I do see it as a game! A game in which I play against the consumer machine that tries to squeeze every cent it can out of me and in which I try to get every bit of value out of it.

I put some great music on, get my Income Statement out, and go through each and every line, asking the following juice-squeezer questions:

- Do I really need this?

- Do I actually use this?

- Do I get maximum value from this specific expense?

- How else can I get the same thing, feeling, or experience—only cheaper?

- Is this taking me closer to my Financial Freedom Vision?

Each month, review your Expenditure in each category and see how large the gap is: how far are you from your target? This will tell you how well you're managing your money.

When you've got your chunks of spending under control, you can just check once a month that you're within your spending targets and then, say, every six months, do a detailed review.

My hubby, Dave, and I do this every six months. We get all our information together, open a bottle of wine, put on some motivating music, and get stuck in. We first tell each other about why we love being financially free, what our exciting plans and goals are for the next few years, and why controlling our spending is so awesome, because it enables us to have the freedom to do whatever we really want.

In this state of mind, we then go through every Expenditure item and challenge it. By doing so, we've managed to keep the positive gap between our Income and Expenditure at over 50 percent for the past eight years while still living full, exciting, and abundant lives with a fantastic standard of living. We simply get rid of what we don't get value from. And we've learned to become expert buyers, ensuring we never pay more than we need to for what we want.

The benefit of tracking each and every month is that you catch yourself quickly before you go too far off target—and it allows you to do something about it. It also allows you to see when you're doing well: if each and every month you see the gap closing, your motivation soars and your Wealth Feast Vision becomes stronger and stronger.

I'm often asked why I bother with a few dollars here and there. It's not about penny pinching: living a small, mean life is neither an abundant nor wealthy life. I bother to record and acknowledge small amounts, because of the combined principles of consciousness and compounding

Consciousness is about control and choice. It's about acknowledging that I am responsible for every outcome in my life and that I have a choice to do whatever I want with my money, knowing that some choices will create my Financial Freedom Feast and some will destroy it. Either way, it's my choice, and I'm very conscious about my spending.

Compounding is about acknowledging that every cent is a seed and every dollar is a golden egg and has a value. If I choose, I can let it hatch and grow into a big feast.

So yes, I do bother with small amounts. I'm also sometimes asked why I don't necessarily stay in the most expensive hotels and so forth. Again, it's about a balance of choice, value, and abundance. I love nice things, but I don't need them in my life to feel wealthy.

Wealth is a feeling that comes from inside of me: it comes from knowing that I value the money in my life. I feel wealthy knowing I now live life on my terms: I get to do the work I love in a way that fulfills me. I am immensely grateful for all I have in my life and so I look after it and grow it. But mostly, I manage my money because I have a huge Why: my life's vision is huge, and the legacy I want to leave, the people I want to help, and the difference I want to make in this world need me to be great with money—and so I am.

My Wealth Feast has been created by small amounts of money consistently added to my Wealth Pots, nurtured, and allowed to grow and expand over time, transforming into a feast that now feeds me with abundance each and every day.

It's as Warren Buffet says: "Someone's sitting in the shade today, because someone planted a tree a long time ago."

Where to squeeze

The following are some areas of spending where most people can squeeze out between 10 percent and 30 percent without reducing their standard of living:

- **Bank fees**—change to a low-cost bank account

- **Interest payments**—destroy your debt

- **Insurances**—in Chapter 13 we will totally nail this. You'll learn how to save significantly on your life, home, car, and medical insurance. With one private client, I found 16 percent savings in just this one area alone!

- **Utilities**—consolidate your utility provision to fewer providers and negotiate a saving.

- **Magazines**—get annual subscriptions for the magazines you really read and get value from and never buy them from the corner shop again. Subscriptions will save you up to 70 percent of the cover costs. Better yet, agree with your family to give magazine subscriptions to each other as gifts.

- **Culinary comfort**—stop buying prepackaged, ready-made and take-away meals. Not only are they full of preservatives and additives, this "convenience" costs you over 120 percent more than the basic ingredients! When you cook, double the quantity and freeze the extra amount, ensuring you already have your own pre-prepared meals available for when you don't have the time or inclination to cook.

- **Gym memberships**—if you use the gym, fantastic, but in fact, fewer than 87 percent of people regularly go. Cancel the membership and rather go exercise in your local park!

- **Other memberships and subscription programs**—look through your direct debits and question whether you use them all.
  Other expense-slashing tips include:

- Buy a filter for your tap water instead of drinking bottled water.

- Challenge the grand double-shot skinny no-foam latte culture! How much are you spending on concepts that barely existed 15 years ago? Do you really need that cappuccino every day?

- Take your own lunch to work.

- Make your hair coloring last longer than you normally would. Instead of getting it done eight times a year, for example, have it done five times.

- Know the different times when your landline and mobile phone rates are at their cheapest and also use Skype, whenever possible.

- Turn off appliances and use low-energy bulbs to reduce your electricity bill.

- Install solar heating in your house.

- Maintain and service your car regularly.

- Turn down the temperature on your water heater.

- Go to movies on discount days.

- Get out books from your local library.

- Start a book club.

- Eat fruit and vegetables that are in season.

- Make your own cleaning products—they're cheaper and better for you and the environment!

- Go to restaurants that let you bring your own wine.

- Do your monthly grocery shopping online with prepared lists.

- Buy generic products.

- Ride to work. Buy a low-cost scooter, or better yet, a bicycle to get to work!

- Set your pool filter, if you have one, to run during off-peak electricity times.

- Buy your household items on sale and from bulk wholesalers.

- Use the Internet to find out about prices and values before you buy.

- Never buy a new car! It loses up to 20 percent of its value as soon as you drive it off the showroom floor.

- Check out charity shops, secondhand merchants, and garage sales.

- Consider giving up some of your vices: smoking, alcohol, gambling, sweets, and chocolate.

- Christmas, Eid al-Adha, and Diwali are not emergencies! Spend half as much as usual on these holidays. Talk openly with your family and friends and share with them your vision for financial freedom.

- Use your ATM card only a planned number of times in the month to withdraw the cash you need.

- Once a month have a no-money Sunday. This is a fun day where each person must come up with an idea of having a fab day without spending anything. Make and fly a kite, have a picnic, watch airplanes, walk in a forest.

- Finally, make your own list of cost-saving ideas. Get the whole family involved. There are also a number of great websites that deal in expense reduction. Surf the net and get inspired! Once you start, you'll be amazed at how much extra money you can find without reducing your standard of living.

Can you stand the heat?

Slashing your Expenses is only one part of squeezing all of the juice out of your Income and reducing your cost of living. Your spending habits are the other.

I promised to share with you the greatest tool in your kitchen that will help you make all of this so much easier. But before I can do that, I need to find out if you can stand the heat!

I'm a trained fire-walking instructor and have walked across blistering hot coals countless times. I've also walked on broken glass, broken wooden boards, and concrete planks with my hands (and taught hundreds of other people how to do the same), I've bent iron bars with my neck and pushed long needles through my hands. Now, before you run screaming and reach for the off button, don't panic: I won't be asking you to walk on hot coals—well, not yet! These activities, in and of themselves, serve no purpose other than as metaphors to experience what we all can do in the right state of mind—and to help us understand the following: you can master the most powerful tool you have—your mind.

In order to master our minds, we need to know how they work and how they process information. I'm sure you've had the experience of a group of people participating in the same event but having completely different responses to it. People read things differently; we all experience a unique and distorted reality. If we don't understand this, then we'll believe that our representation is the actual ("true") reality.

I'm sure you're also familiar with the saying "S***
happens!" Well, it's events that happen. Whether they're
good or bad depends on the interpretation you decide
to put on them. Any and every event has no meaning
other than the meaning we give it. The meaning you
give something, and how you choose to respond to it,
determines the quality and the wealth of your life.

When awake, we register around 2.3 million bits of
information per second. In the film *What the Bleep*, Dr.
Joe Spencer estimates, however, that we're bombarded
with approximately 400 billion bits of data each second.
Now, whether it's 2.3 million or 400 billion, it's certainly
a huge amount! These bits of data are absorbed
primarily through our five senses.

This is too much to cope with consciously, so our
mind sieves the information and filters it down to just
five to nine chunks of information at any given time.
It does this in order for us to make sense of them and,
in so doing, creates an internal representation of the
event. So what we end up with is a representation of
the event, not the event itself.

There are three ways our mind sieves the data coming
in. We delete, distort, and generalize the information to
create our Unique Internal Representation of the event.
Just how we delete, distort, and generalize the data
depends on our beliefs, values, memories, language,
self-imposed rules, meta-programs, and, the strongest
one of all—our identity.

These interweave to create the sieves through which all our world experience is sieved, deleted, distorted, and generalized into a form to which we can give meaning. The issue here isn't that we delete, distort, or generalize. The problem is the quality of these sieves and the meaning we attribute to them.

We then take actions based on the meaning we've chosen to give something and the state of our emotions at that time. These actions then determine the results we get in our lives.

Our emotions are driven by three molders of meaning: our physiology, our focus, and our language. How we use any one of these molders changes the emotion we have toward our internal representation—which, in turn, changes the actions we take, and so, changes the results.

In relation to wealth and every other aspect of life, it's these two power forces, meaning and emotion, that drive the actions we take, and thus determine the results we get. So, if you're not happy with the financial results in your life, change your sieves and your molders!

You need to have a combined set of sieves, physiology, focus, and language to support your Financial Freedom Vision and goal. In life, there are things that we just have to do, such as managing our money. Now, we can either moan about it or we can celebrate it. Celebrating has a completely different energy, and there's also a different energy for receiving, whether it be money, love, or success. It's about yin and yang. Negative thoughts about paying presuppose that you have issues about receiving money. Negative thoughts about managing your money presupposes you have issues about having money to manage in the first place!

Most people say, "I'll believe it when I see it, "but that isn't how it works. Thanks to your sieves, you'll see it when you believe it! And in order to see your financial freedom, you have to believe that it's a reality for you. People who "just seem to succeed" have already installed a series of beliefs and values that allow them to do so, and people who are wealthy have also installed a series of beliefs and values that allow them to make, keep, and grow their money.

Two great techniques for mastering your molders

Since this is so key, I want you to learn two great techniques for mastering your molders of meaning, physiology, focus, and language. You've already started fine-tuning your wealth focus with your teeth-brushing questions. Yep, we really can install great daily habits that, over time, will shift our focus to wealth! So here's a new focus daily habit to add to your new life of wealth.

Every morning, start your day off consciously thinking about your financial freedom life. As you get up, close your eyes and see your financial freedom life as you have designed it. You are already there. Make it a strong and powerful vision in your mind's eye and physically step into it. Experience what it feels like to be in it. Each day, make it stronger and stronger, enjoying how it feels to be financially free.

Language is another molder of meaning. Your words affect your reality and they significantly impact your wealth. Notice the effect of the words "I can't afford it!" or "I don't have the money." Do you use these words? Just how disempowering are they? They simply shut down possibilities and take away your creativity. They constrict your power. If you're choosing not to buy something, rather say, "I choose not to spend my money on this." How about, "My freedom is more important than this, and so I choose my freedom."

Better still, ask yourself the following questions: "How can I afford it? What can I do to afford it? How can I have what I want without spending that amount of money?"

Now, this is starting to get into the realm of quality questions. Remember, our experience of an event is inside us, not outside, and our unconscious cannot differentiate between what's real and what's imagined. So if you're going to make stuff up, you may as well make stuff up that works!

Your Conscious Spending Sieve

Let's go back to the Wealth Kitchen tool that is going to help you make your spending so much richer. I'm talking about the sieve that you created in the last section. Huh? Yep—you created a sieve and you didn't even know it! This is your new sieve: your Conscious Spending Sieve—through which you will test your spending in order to see if your spending is adding to your life or reducing the quality of it. This sieve will help you separate the wheat from the chaff and will also help you remember, when you implement the changes that you're going to make, that you're not saying "no" to anything—you're saying "yes" to your greatest dreams!

Your Conscious Spending Sieve makes you really aware of your spending, and so helps you on your way to your goals. It helps with easier, better decision making when it comes to purchases or investments or what to let go of. From now on, everything goes through the sieve, and everything gets filtered through the sieve of your Big Why and your Financial Freedom Feast Vision, okay?

Your Financial Freedom Vision and your Big Why are actually a powerful set of values that are important to you. And you now know that one of the ways you delete, distort, and generalize is through your values. So instead of just letting it happen unconsciously, you're now going to do it consciously.

You do this by asking yourself:

- "Is this supporting my financial freedom or not?"

- "If I choose to buy this, will it fill my Wealth Pots or empty them?"

- "Does this support my Big Why or take me further away from my dreams?"

- "Will this money choice help me fly higher?"

You'll get your answer immediately. Very few things are needs. Most things are wants. And everything is a choice. Now, here's the thing: this isn't about deprivation (which isn't wealthy); this is about ensuring that your money fulfills you and that the things you choose to spend it on give you value, fill your life, and light you up.

A TIP

- Write the questions on a little card and then slip it into your wallet or purse. Each time you're about to spend money, have a quick run-through of the questions. You'll be amazed by the results.

This filter isn't just for the Necessities Pot; it's for all your Pots. When you spend your Fun Pot, run your choices through your sieve. When you spend your Growth Pot, run your choices through your sieve. Use the power sieves and tools in your head to create your financial freedom. Value yourself by getting the maximum enjoyment and value out of your money.

Your goal as a Wealth Chef is to be conscious of all your actions, including your spending. It's about taking back your power, being in control of your own destiny, and knowing that you get the most out of each decision you make. People tend to believe that our destiny is created at the big milestones in our lives, at the big decisions we have to make. This just isn't so. Our destiny is created in the moment-by-moment decisions we make every day. So make those decisions count!

Review the juice squeezing and sieving techniques below and commit to incorporating some or all of them into your Wealth Cooking:

- **Stop before you buy.** If you've seen an absolutely must-have item, *stop*! Write down what it is, note the price, and take a photo of it with your cell phone. Leave the store, go home, and think about it overnight. When you get home, write out ten ways you can get the money for the item without using your credit card or robbing from your other pots. Determine what value you're going to get from the item. Remember to answer all the questions above. If you do this, the odds are that when morning comes, you'll have decided you don't really need the purchase! If you do still want it, and you can pay for it without dipping into your other pots, then go for it. Using this technique also eliminates buyer's regret.

- **Leave your wallet at home.** Revel in the power of being able to appreciate looking at things without having to have them. Advertisers are brilliant at using all the emotional triggers and persuasion techniques to make you believe you absolutely have to have something that 15 minutes ago you didn't even know existed. Enjoy this experience! You may be amazed at the power you feel by being able to wander around a whole shopping mall and emerge without having bought anything. Try the challenge and enjoy beating the marketers at their own game.

- **Become a master of persuasion.** Read Robert Caldini's brilliant book *Influence: The Psychology of Persuasion.* Understand the powerful techniques marketers and advertisers use to get you to part with your money. These include: the Expensive = Good stereotype, where prices are inflated to make an item seem more desirable, and then discounting it to make it seem like a bargain; the contrasting principle, where an overpriced item is presented first to lessen the perceived cost of subsequent cheaper items; the scarcity technique, where a "special offer" is available for five days only; or the bulk-value illusion ("Buy three for the price of two").

- **Take your name off** mailing lists, e-mail lists, and mail-order catalog lists. Catalogs, especially, provide unnecessary temptation.

- **Always think about the value** of the purchase versus the effort required to earn the after-tax money you're about to spend.

- **Buy Assets instead of just spending!** The truth is you have a finite amount of money that you will earn in your lifetime. The wonderful thing about the modern world is that you have control over how much money you create and how much money you spend. You can change your financial situation whenever you choose! Nevertheless, you still have only so many years to earn money in your lifetime. If you give too much of it away, you won't have enough left over to create your Wealth Feast. It's simple math.

The One-Week Challenge

Are you ready to really take this to a new level? Then try the One-Week Challenge.

The One-Week Challenge consists of making this week a big money "sugar rush" cutback week. Only spend on items in your Security Soup. Now, if even just the thought of this made you stop breathing, then you definitely need it! This is your Wealth Detox.

Do you think you could manage this for just one week?

Squeeze the juice out of every bit of money you spend. Build a strong squeezing muscle by understanding your spending habits and changing them to habits that stock your.

And let go of guilt. It doesn't work. Let go of "shoulds" and "should nots." Just run your intended purchase through your Big Why Sieve and ask those simple quality questions.

Choose freedom. And then choose it again. And again and again! Enjoy finding the treasure already in your life and putting it to work on your Financial Freedom Feast.

11

Wealth Recipe #2:
Expand Your Dough

So, how are your Wealth Pots looking?

- Did you create a fun set to keep at home, to remind you of your increasing wealth?

- Did you accept my challenge and have a money detox?

- Did you cut out all spending and only spend on your Security Soup needs?

- And finally, your language: are you aware of how you're talking? Did you use some of those great "Quality Questions" to ensure that you receive massive value from what you buy?

Speaking of buying stuff, you're now going to learn how to stock your Asset Drawer with stocks and shares in the easiest, simplest, and most effortless way. Oh yes, you get to spend money on the gift for yourself that just keeps on giving!

You'll be learning all about the stock market and how to invest in it, making the process easy and practically automatic, so you can have Assets working for you. You're also going to be putting the Wealth Spices to work on your money, making it work hard so that someday you won't have to!

In the previous chapter, you learned that your first slice of the pie, the very first piece of Income that comes into your life, gets to stay in your life and goes straight into your investment pot.

You also learned that:

- You have a right to keep some of what you earn!

- You have a right to make some of what you earn work for you!

- You have a right to keep on making what that money earns work for you, too!

Okay, okay, it's not just a right; it's a must.

Easier said than done? Perhaps you really want your wealth pie carving to really happen in your life but (as is the case with many people) there just isn't any money left over after you've finished paying everyone else.

You see, therein lies the problem: you pay everyone else first. You are minding everyone else's business except your own.

In other words, you're putting everyone and everything else ahead of you and your goals. If this is happening in your Wealth Cooking, then there's a good chance it's also happening elsewhere in your life.

Remember, you and your wealth should be the most important Expenditure for you, every month.

Even if you're unsure as to whether you'll have enough money to cover your other bills, you must still pay yourself first.

You see, when you do this, you not only trigger that magical wealth accelerator—compounding—you also increase your own self-worth and self-esteem by valuing yourself enough to keep some of what you earn.

In addition, you trigger your imagination, resourcefulness, and creativity to either generate more Income to pay for your bills or reduce your cost of living. Commit now, therefore, to making yourself the most important bill you need to pay each and every month.

Now you're going to learn how to get that investment pot working for you in the easiest, most effortless, and most automatic way possible! Wealth Recipe #2—Expand Your Dough is all about keeping some of the money you've earned and investing it in an environment where it can flourish, undisturbed, so it can do what money is meant to do: grow for you.

- Recipe #2 -
Expand Your Dough

The Expand Your Dough Recipe, like Recipe #1, is so simple that many people fail to believe that this is all they require to become financially free. But it works! Here it is:

- Step 1

    - **Invest a fixed amount of money every month** into a stock market–based fund via an online investment platform.

    - To do this, simply **set up an automatic investment plan** where money is withdrawn automatically and regularly from your bank account and invested in a stock market-based fund on your behalf.

- Step 2

    - **Reinvest any investment returns.** Any Income the investment pays out must be automatically reinvested.

    - Most funds have either an Income or an accumulation option. **Select the accumulation option,** which automatically puts the Income back into your Asset pot and just buys more of the fund for you.

- Step 3

    - **Leave it alone to grow.**

- Step 4

    - **Once a year, increase your monthly contribution,** either in the same fund or in a new fund, in order to build up a portfolio of funds.

- Step 5

  - **Leave it alone to grow.**

That's it. I told you it was easy!

The Automatic Investment Plan

These are the advantages of your automatic investment plan (AIP):

1. You only have to "think and act" once.

2. You can track and manage it anytime, night or day, online.

3. You benefit from Dollar Cost Averaging (see this section further on in the book).

4. You benefit from lower investment costs, thus putting more money in your Asset Drawer (see this section further on in the book).

5. Your AIP has more money added every month, automatically.

It's fun to watch your Wealth Feast grow!

Your Asset Wealth Pantry drawer gets filled by itself, and so your Net Worth increases.

Now, let's break this down a bit.

Decide the amount of money you're going to invest every month from Pot 1—your Investment Pot—into your AIP. "Why a regular fixed amount each month?" you may ask.

Well, a fixed regular investment triggers another great Wealth Cooking process, called:

Dollar cost averaging

Cost averaging works as follows: each month, you invest a fixed amount of money, and that money buys a number of units in the fund that you've chosen. The number of units you receive each month depends on the price of the units on the day you buy them. When the price of the units goes up, you receive fewer units, and when the price of the units goes down, you receive more. Over time, the average cost of all the units you've bought will be lower than the average price of the fund's units over the same period.

If your eyelid remote control has just triggered, and you're starting to switch off, please come back! This section is the one where you need to become aware, above all, of any tendency you may have for Analysis Paralysis. Yes, that Wealth Feast-destroying sickness that causes us to sit on fences instead of making decisions, to lose opportunities because we keep telling ourselves we need to know, to understand it a bit more, first. The best way to learn is by doing. And the best way to go about it is to start by committing yourself to increasing your financial literacy and knowledge as you go.

About the dollar cost averaging: it isn't essential that you understand exactly how or why it works; you just need to know that it's good for your wealth. Obviously, I'm not telling you to blindly follow everything I'm saying—I'm just saying that sometimes you can move forward with only a broad understanding. I don't know about you, but I only have a broad knowledge of my car's power steering system, for example, but this doesn't prevent me from using my car or hamper my driving pleasure!

Besides the lower average price of the units, there is an additional great factor to cost averaging: you don't have to worry about the ups and downs of the stock market—known as volatility—or trying to time when to buy. Timing the market is when you try to buy low and sell high. And trying to time the market by jumping in and out means keeping a constant eye on events— not to mention the fact that we'll probably get our timing wrong more often than not, anyway! Trying to time the markets is an octopus strategy, often ending up in Analysis Paralysis and your doing nothing.

Cost averaging is also great because you actually get all excited when the market goes down! While others are panicking and diving off the cliff like a bunch of lemmings, you can celebrate, knowing you're getting more for your money. Remember, you are in this investment for the long term, so you want to buy as many units as possible. Warren Buffet asked, "If you expect to be a net investor during the next five years, should you hope for a higher or lower stock market during that period?"

Many investors get this one wrong. Even though they're going to be net buyers of stocks for years to come, they're elated when stock prices rise and depressed when they fall. This reaction makes no sense. Only those who will be sellers of shares in the near future should be happy at seeing stocks rise. Buyers want sinking prices. You want the stock exchange to be having a massive sale when you're investing. You want to buy when the price is going down, because you'll get more and, in the long term (when the unit price has grown), you'll end up with a better return.

Select the fund of your choice and set up your AIP.

Research online brokers and open an investment account. Compare the costs, flexibility, and options available from different online investment brokers and investment platforms in your country.

AIPs are easy to set up. Most unit trust and exchange traded fund (ETF) providers also have regular investment plans that you can subscribe to. It's simplest and cheapest to set up your AIP online, but you can also do so through a financial adviser.

So, what should you buy?

I recommend you start your equity investing in a unit trust or ETF. The objective of your AIP is to keep it simple: low investment costs, very little management required from you, and risk kept at a minimum.

When you buy a unit trust or an ETF, you're actually buying a piece of a whole basket of shares. You don't have to select the individual shares, and your investment is spread across all the shares in the fund you buy, which automatically diversifies your investment. In other words, the risk of your investment going down due to one individual share going down is diluted significantly.

I also recommend that you invest in an index tracker fund. Why an index tracker? Back to my investing hero, Mr. Buffett: the best advice Buffett has for small investors is to put their money into an index tracker Fund because of its broad diversification and low costs. To quote: "A very low-cost index is going to beat a majority of the amateur-managed money and professionally managed money funds."

The index tracker

As investors, there are only two things that we can control: the fees we pay and the Assets we invest in.

An index tracker is a low-cost, simple investment fund that mimics the performance of the stock market. In order to understand how it works, it's useful to know a little about stock market indexes: an index is a method of tracking how well a stock market, or a particular sector of it, is performing. It enables investors to assess how well they're doing by comparing their own performance against it. They can see if they're out-performing (doing better than the index) or under-performing (doing worse).

Each index is made up of many different companies. When you hear on the news that "The Dow Jones is down 100 points" or the "Footsie has risen 50 points today," the news anchor is referring to the stock market indexes of the New York Stock Exchange and the London Stock Exchange, respectively. But what does a rise of 50 points actually mean?

Say the index rises by 50 points, from 5,000 to 5,050, or one percent. This means that the value that the stock market is placing on all of the companies within that exchange index has gone up by one percent.

The price of each company is determined by the buying and selling of its shares on that specific day. There are literally hundreds of different indexes across the world. As well as tracking the markets of whole countries, there are also indexes that track individual industries or sectors, such as retail, industrial, or property, or large geographical regions such as Europe, Africa, or the East.

In the United States, the main indexes are the Dow Jones Industrial Average (the Dow), the Standard & Poor's (the S&P), and the Nasdaq (where most technology shares are listed). In the United Kingdom, it's the FTSE, which tracks the performance of the largest companies listed on the London Stock Exchange, and in Australia the main index is the ASX: the Australian Stock Exchange. Other indexes you'll come across include the Nikkei (Japan), the Hang Seng (Hong Kong), the Dax (Germany), the CAC (France), and the JSE (South Africa).

An index tracker is a fund that holds shares in the same proportion as a specific index. So a FTSE 100 tracker, for instance, attempts to mimic the performance of the 100 largest companies listed on the London Stock Exchange. When the components of an index change, the index tracker will adjust its holdings accordingly. An index tracker, therefore, differs from most other funds—collectively referred to as managed funds—where it's the fund manager who decides when and which companies are bought and sold.

Whether index trackers are better than managed funds is a cause of fierce debate in the world of investment. For me, the evidence is fairly clear-cut, as it shows that index trackers beat the vast majority of managed funds over the long term.

A study by research firm WM Company found that 82 percent of managed funds failed to beat the market (the index) over the course of twenty years. While you may think that sounds bad, it's actually even worse, because this figure only includes funds that survived for the entire twenty years.

Many poorly performing funds are shut down or simply merged into other funds. This means that the chances of picking a fund now that will do worse than the market over the next twenty years is likely to be a great deal higher than 82 percent, and it is probably, in fact, well in excess of 90 percent.

John Bogle, founder of the U.S.-based fund giant Vanguard, backs this up. Bogle looked at the returns of investing $10,000 over a 25-year period: if you'd invested the money in an actively managed retail fund 25 years ago, your $10,000 would have grown to $48,200. However, putting the same amount into a broad index-tracking fund with low fees would have grown it to $170,800—a huge difference of $120,000!

This difference is made up of high fees, kickback commissions to advisers, costs associated with churning of the portfolio (which is when the fund manager buys and sells too much), and poor market timing.

Some people believe that it's possible to consistently pick one of the few funds that will beat the index. I don't want to spend all my time following every managed fund and every fund manager to make sure I select the few funds that beat the index, and this is why I like index trackers.

Buffett also warns investors to "Beware the glib helper who fills your head with fantasies while he fills up his pockets with fees." In my view, a vast majority of the financial industry is made up of these glib helpers!

So why do managed funds perform so badly as a group?

Taken together, managed funds are, essentially, the market. This means that collectively, they hold their investments in pretty much the same proportion as an index tracker does. Before taking costs into account, therefore, you'd expect a managed fund and an index tracker to produce the same sort of return. When you take costs into account, however, two key differences emerge between index trackers and managed funds.

First, charges for managed funds tend to be a lot higher than those for index trackers. A typical managed fund charges around 1.5 percent a year, whereas the average index tracker charges around 0.5 percent and some charge even less. These differences may sound small, but they compound each year and give index trackers a huge advantage over the long term.

The second difference is that managed funds trade more frequently. The typical managed fund turns over around 50 percent of its holdings each year, meaning that the fund manager buys and sells at least half of the stocks in the fund each year. Each buy or sell, called a "trade," costs money.

The dealing costs associated with this trading activity give managed funds an additional handicap to overcome when pitched against index trackers, which tend to have an annual portfolio turnover of less than 20 percent.

If an index tracker were to perform, say, 1.5 percentage points better each year than a managed fund because of the lower costs, what difference could this make to you?

Let's say you put $1,000 into a tracker and $1,000 into a managed fund. The index tracker grows at 10 percent a year; the managed fund at 8.5 percent a year. After ten years, your managed fund would be worth $2,261, but your tracker would be worth $2,594. Over twenty years, the managed fund would grow to $5,112 and the tracker would be worth $6,728. So your extra 1.5 percent return a year results in 24 percent more cash for you at the end of twenty years!

In addition to a higher expected return, index trackers have one final major advantage over managed funds: they are much simpler to operate. Essentially, you just pick your tracker and leave it to do its job for twenty years or even longer.

If you prefer the managed fund route, however, not only do you have a bewildering number to choose from in the first place (several thousand, in fact!), but you also have to continually monitor the fund's performance and even pick another fund should its returns fail to inspire or its manager departs for elsewhere (a fairly common occurrence).

All things considered, I believe that an index tracker is the most suitable initial investment vehicle for the Wealth Chef and the ideal place to start your equity investing.

Three simple steps

These are the three simple steps to set up your AIP:

1. Commit to a specific amount to pay yourself.

2. You can start an AIP with most investment houses with very small regular investment amounts.

3. Just be aware of your trading versus investment costs. Remember that the habit of paying yourself

first is more important than the specific amount of money right now.

As you see the money grow in your investment account, your motivation to add more will increase. And once you've mastered Recipes #1 and #4 (the Debt Destroyer), you'll realize you can increase the amount significantly, without lowering your standard of living.

Select your index tracker fund

Choosing an index tracker is relatively simple. There are three main things to consider:
- Which index it tracks
- What type of fund it is: unit trust or ETF
- The charges

I suggest that you start with the primary index for the country you live in. From there, you can add trackers for other geographic regions and sectors.

Your target will be to have four or five different trackers in your whole portfolio.

What type of fund?

Most index trackers are either unit trusts or ETFs. Unit trusts are priced daily and can be bought directly from a fund manager, via an online discount broker or financial adviser.

Experts have found that two factors, cost and Asset class, determine the bulk of our investing returns. This is the reason I'm a big fan of ETFs, which are ultra-low-cost index funds that trade on the share market, just like other shares.

ETFs are traded on the stock market and, therefore, their prices change continuously throughout the trading day.

More and more, index trackers are becoming available through the huge growth of the ETF industry.

Your decision as to whether you go for a unit trust or an ETF should be based on ease of investment and costs.

Two types of funds

There are two types of funds you can select: Income Funds and Accumulation Funds.

Income Funds are set up so that when Income is earned by an investor, the fund manager pays that Income out to the investor in the form of a cash payment. In the case of shares and funds, the Income is a result of dividends being paid out by the companies that you own in the fund. While you're building your Wealth Feast, you do not want this paid out.

Accumulation Funds, on the other hand, automatically reinvest all Income earned by an investor back into the fund. This is usually reflected in an increase in the unit or share price of the fund.

Funds make the distinction between Income and Accumulation status in two different ways: some funds have two separately created and operated funds (e.g., XYZ Growth Fund Income and XYZ Growth Fund Accumulation). In other cases, there's just one fund and you make a selection of either reinvesting your Income or having your Income paid to you in cash.

Automatic reinvestment is also cheaper, as you don't get charged broker fees or transaction costs for the reinvestment. Keeping your investment costs as low as possible is another Wealth Chef skill—Financial Competence.

What about investment property? Yes, the same reinvestment recipe applies: all net Income you earn from your investment property must be reinvested back into your Wealth Feast!

Make your Wealth Kitchen a bustling, happy place full of little Wealth Chefs in the form of your investment returns, whipping up your feast for you. And please don't kill these wonderful workers by robbing yourself!

What are the costs?

When selecting your specific index tracker, look carefully at all the costs involved: look at the total expense ratio (TER) of the fund you're considering. You should be selecting a fund with a TER of 0.5 percent or less.

Also look at your trading costs. This means the cost of buying the fund. Keep your average trading cost as low as you can by selecting an online trading/investing platform with competitive costs and by buying your investment in big enough lumps to keep the percentage cost of each trade less than one percent

Complete the application forms and start your AIP.

You can start your AIP with most of the major funds online. Get the forms, fill them in, and get going! Also, make sure you set up a direct debit from your bank account on the day after your Income comes in, so that you're paying yourself first.

AIPs are given different names by different institutions. Don't worry about the name, just do it! Simply decide how much money you're going to pay yourself each month, select your online platform, select your index to track, set up your AIP, and commit to it.

With regards to paying yourself, if this is new to you and you're still getting to grips with reducing your cost of living (not the standard of living), I recommend that you set up your AIP direct debit directly from your main bank account. Keep it simple.

If, however, you want to start building up your savings pot and additional investment capital to, say, put a down payment on an investment property in addition to your AIP, you should open up an investment account separate from your everyday banking account. Set up an automatic transfer from the bank account where your Income gets deposited into your investment and savings account.

Set it up for the day after the Income is deposited. This transfer must include your AIP monthly investment amount, as well as your additional investment and savings amounts. Your monthly AIP direct debit is then set up from your investment account.

Just make sure that the bank fees associated with the additional account justify this strategy and that you won't be able to dip into this account easily!

If you really want to accelerate your investment fund have your Income deposited into your investment savings account and then set up an automatic transfer from your investment account to your everyday account for exactly the amount of money you have budgeted to live on. This way, any increase in your Income or bonus payment goes into your investment pot and you keep living happily off the same budget that you've already set up.

Don't rob yourself!

Now, the key to making this really work for you is: don't rob yourself, reinvest your investment returns!

Imagine going to an ATM, withdrawing money, and then putting a gun to your own head and forcing yourself to hand the money over to the first person you can find. Yes, as ridiculous as it sounds, most people have mastered the art of robbing themselves.

How do they do this? They start off well: they set up an investment plan just as in Recipe #2 and invest a little money. Then it all comes to a grinding halt when they sabotage their entire Freedom Feast: as soon as the money is doing what it's meant to do—that is, making more money—they rob their wealth pot and give it to the first retailer they can find.

If you're baking a cake and keep opening the oven door to check on it, taste it, and see how it's doing, you soon end up with a flat flop! Well, money is just the same: if you spend your investment returns too early, you remove the power of compounding and take yourself right back to a Break-even Money Cook.

Wealth Chefs have mastered the recipe of letting their money do exactly what it's meant to do. They see every dollar as a seed to be planted to earn hundreds more, which can then be replanted to earn thousands more.

Expanding dough only works effectively as a long-term plan and it requires compounding and time to work its magic and transform your little contributions into a magnificent feast.

Am I saying you are never to spend the money being generated in your AIP? Well, yes and no.

In the short term, you won't be touching your AIP contributions nor the money it earns.

In the long term, this becomes your Freedom Feast, and you'll be feasting off it happily, once it has grown to a size where it can sustain itself. The money you invest in your AIP is the Foundation of your Freedom Feast. It needs to remain in your wealth pot so it can grow.

Please understand that contributing to your AIP for a couple of years isn't going to change your life. However, contributing to your AIP and reinvesting *all* your investment returns until your AIP has reached your identified Financial Freedom Feast Net Worth will change your financial life forever!

The most exciting thing about mastering Expand Your Dough is that it accelerates your wealth growth and will allow you to retire early and feed yourself from your Freedom Feast for the rest of your life. By reinvesting all your investment returns, you're creating a whole army of little Wealth Chefs to do the hard work for you.

Letting your money work and reinvesting your investment returns is a critical component of this recipe, which you need to master for your long-term wealth success.

Congratulations!

Congratulations, you are just three more recipes away from becoming a Wealth Chef!

Just this recipe alone will make you significantly richer. Each and every month, your Asset Wealth Pantry drawer will be getting fuller and fuller and you'll be able to rest assured that you're creating your Financial Freedom Feast.

Start today. Every dollar you pay yourself first and invest in your AIP will start working hard for you, so that you don't have to!

Expand Your Dough

LEVEL OF DIFFICULTY > Easy

. . . .

INGREDIENTS:

- Portion of Wealth Pot 1 "Financial Freedom Pot"

- Form-filling
- Mastering the molders of meaning

TOOLS REQUIRED:

- Bank account details
- Online broker account

SKILLS REQUIRED:

- Internet searching

TIME REQUIRED:

- 3 hours initial setup
- 10 minutes a month, to check values
- 1 hour a year to expand and review

METHOD:

. . . .

Step 1 > Invest a fixed amount of money every month into an index tracker fund, via an AIP.

Step 2 > Reinvest any investment returns. Select your preferred accumulation fund option.

Step 3 > Leave it alone to grow.

Step 4 > Once a year, increase your monthly contribution, either in the same tracker or by adding a new index tracker, to build up a portfolio of trackers.

Step 5 > Leave it alone to grow.

. . . .

*Relax, and focus on expanding you
as your wealth grows.*

12.

Wealth Recipe #3: Blitz That Debt!

This is one of my favorite recipes! I love it because after you've learned it, you'll be able to ensure that debt—a source of pain, guilt, and confusion for so many people—never figures again in your life. This is a wealth recipe that, if applied and maintained, will ensure that you're completely free of bad debt in four to seven years' time, no matter what your current level of debt is.

Before we get to shattering your debt, however, how's your dough expansion going? How does it feel to be the owner of another company, actually a few of the top companies in the world? If you haven't yet opened your online investing account and bought your first index tracker, then go back and ask yourself: why not? If you're still waiting until you have all your "money stuff" sorted out, or all your debt is paid off, or until things are just more settled financially, then *stop*.

Understand this: those things will get sorted out once you choose to value yourself, once you choose to

pay yourself and your financial future first. Remember
the combined impact of compounding and time?

Many people, especially women, believe consciously
or unconsciously that investing and owning investments
in their own name is somehow indulgent, or selfish, and
that it's something that must come after they look after
everyone else first. Well, remember the advice when
you fly: first secure your own oxygen mask before you
help others! You can only be the best wife, mother,
daughter, leader, or friend if you fully support yourself.

Because when you're in a place of certainty, and
feeling secure about your money and financial well-
being, then you can really soar and be there for others.

And when it comes to couples, you must both have
investments in your own names. So get your automatic
investment plan (AIP) in place and keep feeding it until
it can feed you!

I also hope you're still brushing those teeth at night
as you contemplate all the things that you're grateful
for, proud of, and excited about!

The meaning of debt

The following recipe may be a bit tough for you,
depending on your current level of debt and the meaning
you choose to give it. Remember, however, that nothing
has any meaning except the meaning that you choose
to give it. No time for guilt and self-flagellation! Those
energies won't help you on your financial freedom
journey!

As you tackle this subject, manage your state of being, notice any negative stuff that may come up, say a nice "thank you" to it, and then let it go, even telling it, "I don't need you today," if that helps. And yes, with a big smile on your face!

Let me ask you a question: when you think about your current level of debt, when you think about all the money that's gone and that you owe, when you think about the interest being charged—what's your main emotion?

For many it is guilt, despair, hopelessness, or even shame. "My dirty little secret" is what one of my clients called it. Now here's another golden nugget I want to share: if you want debt out of your life and destroyed forever, then the key emotional tweak you need to make to destroy debt forever is to turn guilt into anger—yes, you heard me! No *guilt*!!

Nothing has any meaning except the meaning you choose to give it, and you need to give your current debt story a meaning that drives you to take action. There is never a good time for guilt and beating yourself up over it, as those energies don't serve you and certainly don't and won't help you to destroy your debt.

It also isn't about feeling sorry for yourself or for others in debt. Feeling sorry—for yourself or someone else—is an exceptionally disempowering emotion as it presupposes that a person is stuck there.

Instead, turn guilt into anger . . . yes, get really, really angry about all this debt in your life. "Ann, I thought anger was bad," you might be thinking. Here's the thing: guilt, despair, embarrassment, and shame are all shrinking, disempowering emotions that drain us of our power. They are also static emotion—just experience what they feel like in your body; they tend to make you slump, go inside yourself, and freeze. Anger, on the other hand, is an extremely powerful emotion, and we need power to blast through and destroy this debt.

So, get angry! If you're still unsure as to how to do that and have been practicing guilt and shame, then go back to your Big Why and use the following three power questions to turn guilt into anger.

You can also write these questions out and have them available to you when you're considering putting more stuff on the same credit cards you want to destroy.

The three power questions

The three power questions to getting really angry:

1. **What is this debt costing you in hard-earned money?** With most credit cards, if you only pay the minimum monthly payment, you'll spend close to four times more than what you thought you paid for the original item. If you knew that that pair of boots was going to cost four times the price on the tag, would you still have bought them? What about those items you bought on sale for 25 percent off that will actually cost you 250 percent more? Or how about that holiday that went on the credit card, now knowing that it's actually costing you

four more holidays just like it, which you will never be able to take? And how about that flat-screen TV you're still paying for? I hope you're starting to get angry at how much that stuff is actually costing you. It's not only the four times multiplier that robs you; it's also the time. The average credit card would take 15 to 20 years to pay off if you only made the minimum payment. That's 15 to 20 years of having your past being dragged around with you.

2. **What is that debt costing you in lost opportunity— what can't you do because of this debt in your life?**

3. **What is that debt costing those you love?** What can't they do because of this debt you have holding you and them back? What can't they experience because you have this debt sucking away the opportunities and the things they should be able to have, do, and experience?

I hope these three power questions have got you getting angry. Not angry at yourself, but angry at the situation you're in, angry enough to ignite a burning desire to be free of it forever.

Remember, guilt, shame, embarrassment, and despair are not going to help you change your debt situation; in fact, they will more than likely just drive you deeper into debt—so use those three powerful questions to make the most important first emotional tweak you need to make: get angry!

The easy path and the difficult path

I believe each and every one of us has everything she needs in order to manifest or create the most amazing life for herself. But if your wealth isn't yet where you want it to be, then something is blocking you.

There are two paths you can choose: the easy path or the difficult path. Easy is actually difficult and difficult is actually easy. The easy path is the path of no challenge, no growth. It's the one where people say, "I would have . . . if only . . . "The path you've already chosen is the difficult path, the path of taking responsibility for the life you create—so create a life worth living!

Let me share with you the story of Bill. As you know, I trained as a civil engineer and spent twenty-something years working around the world on various amazing infrastructure projects. On one particular construction site I was visiting, I met Nick, an amazing character, and he told me about Bill. Bill worked on a construction site that Nick was supervising. When Bill joined the site, he was assigned to a crew.

At lunch on his first day, he sat down with his new crew and opened his lunch box. As he opened it, he let out a deep sigh and said, "Does anyone want to swap their sandwich with me? I've got sardine sandwiches and I hate them!" No one wanted his sandwich, so he went hungry and grumbled his way through the afternoon.

The next day arrived, and again Bill sat down with the crew and opened his lunch box, and again the same thing happened: "Does anyone want to swap with me? I hate sardine sandwiches!" This happened every day for the whole week. By Friday, one of his workmates was starting to get irritated and asked Bill why he didn't just tell his wife he hated sardine sandwiches and ask her to make a different kind? Bill looked at his lunch box, then at his workmate, confused, and said: "But I make my own lunch."

You may laugh, but in so many areas of our lives we do exactly this! If you don't like what's in your lunch box, you must first acknowledge that you're responsible for packing your own lunch and then change what you put into it! So if there's a lot of bad debt—consumer debt—in your life, then the first step to eliminating it is to take responsibility for it being there in the first place.

Part of doing so is understanding your spending habits.

You've already gone deep into what you've spent your money on in the past, and you've set up your sieves and your Wealth Pots to help you manage your spending in the future, but without understanding the behavior drivers around your spending, real change won't happen.

Spending emotions

Understanding which triggers got you into debt in the first place is key to destroying your current debt and ensuring you don't end up back in the same place. Become aware of why you buy and when you spend and start noticing which emotions are at play when you do so:

- **Do you spend more when you feel insecure, guilty, lonely, bored, hungry, angry, and frustrated?** What's your spending trigger?

- **Do you spend money to reward yourself?** "I've worked hard, so I deserve this massage." How about changing the reward by rewarding yourself with a Wealth Feast that lasts forever?

- **How much of your spending is impulse buying?** Spur of the moment, "Oh I've just got to have that" kind of buying rather than planned spending?

For some people, this may only be a minor financial problem, but for others, it's a disease on the same level as compulsive eating, gambling, or binging. Often these people become depressed over how far they've sunk into debt and vow to change their ways. Unfortunately, the emotions of guilt and self-loathing are the very same ones that drove them to spend in the first place, and so they try to escape these feelings by spending again. And so the vicious cycle continues.

Become aware of your Spending Emotions and the things that trigger impulsive spending for you, as they are absolutely essential to changing your money story.

Do you spend money out of guilt? "I'll buy this for little Johnny because I haven't had much time for him in the last week. He'll love me more if I give him a gift."

I can assure you: little Johnny, your wife or husband, your friends and family, whoever it is you feel you need to buy for will appreciate you much more when you're financially free and you don't have to turn to them for financial support later on in life!

Do you shop impulsively when you need to soothe yourself or make yourself feel more worthy? The irony is that you can feel anything you want, any time you want to, because every emotion comes from inside of us, never from something outside. Use your quality questions about what's great in your life, and what you're proud of and grateful for whenever you need a lift—and notice how the urge to spend disappears.

Do you spend because you believe that some part of you is "not enough"—not skilled enough, not pretty enough, not happy enough, not young enough, or not old enough?

TIPS

- **Practice self-awareness.** Each time you're about to spend money, ask yourself the following questions:
  - "What am I feeling right now?"
  - "What do I believe this purchase will give me?"
  - "Does this purchase add to, or subtract from, my Wealth Feast?"
- **Remember:** your internal representation, together with the three molders of meaning—language, focus, and physiology—result in the emotions you feel that trigger the actions you take. So review all three.

- **Ask yourself: "How am I? Am I hungry or thirsty?"** Change your physiology: if you're hungry when you go food shopping you'll end up spending up to 45 percent more than if you're full when you go! So have a quick snack before you leave the house. This will change your molders of meaning, change your emotions when you shop, change the actions you take—and save you money. It will shorten the distance to your Financial Freedom Feast. Having a shopping list and sticking to it also reduces your ad hoc spending by as much as 84 percent   .

- **Ask yourself: "What am I focusing on?"** "Is my imagination focusing on the short-term pleasure of the things I believe this purchase will give me, or am I focusing on my Wealth Feast?" Change your focus. Get your Wealth Feast Vision back at the forefront of your mind, and remember all the good things you're creating for yourself. Make this picture more powerful than the short-term gratification that has crept into your mind.

- **Ask yourself: "What am I saying to myself about this purchase?"** "Is the language I use helping my goal or impeding it?" Change the words you're using.

- **Be brutally honest with yourself** and write down the answers. After all, you're the one in control of you! You see, our emotions are habitual patterns. We go to those emotions because we've wired ourselves that way. It's only with awareness that we can start changing the patterns that don't work for us. But like a muscle that hasn't been worked for a while, we need to consciously work it and do so over and over again, until we've wired a new path and a new set of habits—which, in turn, trigger new sets of emotions.

Debt

As American showman P.T. Barnum once said "Debt robs a man of his self-respect, and makes him almost despise himself. Grunting and groaning and working for what he's eaten up or worn out, and now, when he's called upon to pay up, he has nothing to show for his money—this is properly termed 'working for a dead horse.'"

Do you owe your life instead of owning it? Then the Debt Destroyer Recipe is the one to get you out of Debtors' Prison!

Debt is by far the greatest financial burden on the average family and the most insidious destroyer of wealth around. In the West, household debt sits at around 85 percent of household Income. The developing world is now rapidly catching up. Today, nearly a quarter of the world's population struggles to keep up with the minimum repayments on their debt. These folk know all about compounding—the problem is that they don't understand it; they just experience it working against them every day, burying them further and further in debt.

Seventy percent of credit card and store card users only pay off the minimum balance each month—which means that banks, retailers, and other card issuers generate massive monthly interest. Credit is a big winner for the banks and lenders and a big loser for the card holders.

Being in debt makes you vulnerable.

The debt that we're talking about here (and the debt you're about to learn how to destroy) is consumer debt. The dictionary definition of "consume" is: "to destroy, squander, waste, or expend." Wow. That's pretty clear! Consumer debt destroys, squanders, wastes, and expends wealth. Sadly, it doesn't just stop there: like a bush fire out of control, debt devours almost everything in its path, destroying not only wealth but also relationships, marriages, and dreams, crushing people's spirits and, in some cases, even their lives.

You may think I am being a bit melodramatic here. I'm not. Consumer debt is the single biggest cause of stress, heartache, and pain in our modern world. It's cited as the number one cause of fights in relationships.

Consumer debt is a prison that people volunteer to go into. In fact, they go in smiling, blissfully unaware of the torture that awaits them and the effect it will have on their lives.

Les's Story

A friend of mine, Les, was enjoying his Dream Life, the high life. He had a quarry business, supplying rock and base material to the construction industry. His monthly Income was huge. He had a shiny Porsche (financed); his wife had an enormous Range Rover; they had a gorgeous five-bedroom home (mortgaged to the hilt), a big BMW GS motorbike (financed) two kids at private schools (funded on bank loans), all the toys you can imagine (bought on his credit cards), and even an airplane (also leased).

Les worked hard and played hard, spending a lot of money along the way. One day, Les went to work to discover that his biggest customer had gone bankrupt and was unable to pay for a huge order that had already been delivered. Les went from a large Income every month to making no money at all. Yet the bills kept coming in.

Like 95 percent of the population, Les wasn't able to survive more than a few months without his Income flowing in. He had to close down his business, firing over six hundred people who relied on him to feed their families. It took him several months to find another job, and when he did, the truth became abundantly clear: he could no longer afford his lifestyle. He was going to lose it all. Worse still, Les hadn't separated his business from his personal finances, and so the few Assets he did have personally, he was also going to lose. So began the worst journey of his life. The shame, stress, and fatigue began to take its toll on Les's body. He literally looked like a doomed man. The worst thing, however, was that Les had volunteered for all this! By financing his life through debt, Les had walked straight into a financial prison. One day, standing in front of a mirror, the truth hit him.

It wasn't the loss of Income that had put him in this situation; it was debt! It was his consumer lifestyle funded by debt, based on money he didn't have, that had caused him such pain. If he'd actually owned the cars, the house, the motorbike, and the airplane, he wouldn't have lost them. If he'd put the money that he'd earned to work, instead of burning it, it wouldn't have mattered if he'd lost his job. His kids' schooling would have been funded from his investments, and he wouldn't have had to experience the shame and sense of failure when he had to explain to them that they had to leave their private school because he could no longer afford the fees.

Les had been living off decades of future income, under the false assumption that his business would always do well, and that he would always be bringing in a large Income and be living the "high life." He also believed his Income would increase, and so, in the future, he'd be able to pay off the debts. He never understood that debt is a habit, so that as Income grows, so does the habit of creating more debt.

I'm sure you have similar stories of friends, family, or maybe even yourself. Even though many people go to university, manage bank accounts, and earn tens of thousands of dollars a year, they've never been taught the Recipes for Wealth. As a result, they offer themselves up as sacrificial lambs to the slaughter, getting themselves into nightmare scenarios that, in most cases, destroy any chance of wealth and freedom for themselves.

After witnessing Les's struggle and that of a number of other people, I did extensive research and discovered the very effective Debt Snowball strategy. I offered to teach it to him, so that he'd be able to pay off everything he owed, including his mortgage, in four to seven years. Les would have to become a great "salesperson": he'd need to sell his cars, his plane, his motorbike—everything but his house. After he had gotten rid of those Liabilities he'd be left with 26 years on his mortgage and lots of credit card debt. I showed him that by using the Debt Snowball method, he'd be able to pay off everything in only four years and seven months!

I also prepared a Financial Freedom Menu for Les and showed him that despite already being in his mid-40s, he could take the same money that he was using for car, house, and credit card payments and add that to his investment pot, buying more Assets, so that by the time he was 61, he and his wife would be financially free.

I wish I could tell you that Les took up my offer. Instead, Les was so locked into his own beliefs and patterns that he refused to even consider it. Despite my showing him the whole plan I'd created specifically for him, he chose to stay stuck.

Les just couldn't stand to sell off his toys and other symbols of what he believed represented success and wealth. He was in total denial as to the role that he'd played in his own downfall. He shouted his story at anyone who would listen, telling them how unfair life was, how the banks were bastards, and how his current situation was the fault of the company that couldn't pay him. Everyone and everything besides himself were to blame. Because he refused to see that he'd got himself into this situation, he couldn't grasp that he was the only one who could get himself out of it!

For many people, being the victim is more comforting and easier in the short term than taking responsibility for the situation they find themselves in. Being the victim may feel good in the moment, but it has absolutely devastating long-term consequences.

As the saying goes, "If you find yourself in a hole, stop digging."

Sadly, Les's story didn't end well. He lost everything, including his house. Initially, his wife stayed with him, but despite her support, he became more and more bitter, losing the job he'd managed to get and eventually losing her, too. The last I heard, Les was working as a groundskeeper for a country estate in the United Kingdom. Alone, bitter, and broke.

It didn't have to be that way. Les's situation could have been the most invigorating and valuable lesson of his entire life, a lesson that would have made him grow and become a better business owner, father, husband—and Wealth Chef as a result! His life could have been an inspiration to others.

I believe our lives can be either an inspiration or a warning—and we get to choose the one it's going to be.

I learned two key lessons from Les: first, debt isn't logical. Trying to implement only logical solutions to an illogical problem doesn't work, and so I refined the Debt Destroyer Strategy to include some totally illogical elements that you'll soon discover.

Second, a person must participate in their own rescue. Even when drowning, they have to reach out and hold on to the life buoy thrown to them. If they don't, you can't help.

I can't describe adequately just how good it feels to own your own life, to know that all your power is within you, to experience the peace that comes from living debt free. You, too, will experience this peace once you learn Wealth Chef Recipe #3!

Ironically, now that I understand debt, I actually have more of it than ever. I owe millions. *But* my debt is *good* debt: it's used to buy Assets. In addition to the wealth accelerator— compounding—I've learned how to use the second wealth accelerator, leveraging (otherwise known as borrowing) to accelerate my wealth. I have loads of intentional, good debt—investment debt— which I use to accelerate my husband's and my wealth.

Just like compounding, debt isn't selective—it's like fire: it can warm you, help you cook your food and your Financial Freedom Feast, and keep you safe and secure, but if misunderstood and not controlled, it can destroy you. And until you've mastered and are effectively eliminating consumer debt, you haven't yet learned how to play with fire—so don't go there!

Why are you in debt?

This isn't about blame and shame. It's about understanding the forces at play and your own drivers, so that you have the power to change it all. If you don't know where you are and how you got there, you can't change!

There's a line in a movie that goes, "He who owns the debt has the power!" I can't remember the movie but I remember thinking that this is a very telling statement. It's true of individuals, companies, and countries: the people, companies, and countries that own the debt of others, own the people, the companies, and the countries. Billions are made on debt. Industries compete to own your debt, companies trade debt, and countries fight to control debt. On an individual level, as soon as you have consumer debt, you've given your power away and you're owned by someone else.

In relation to consumer debt, there are four industries whose sole aim is to get you into debt, so that they have control over you—and, hence, power. It's the mission of these industries to get you into, and hold you in, perpetual and escalating debt.

They are the manufacturers, the advertisers, the banks and lenders, and the financial advisers.

You're worth it!

The manufacturers' job is to create more and more stuff for you to buy, and the advertisers' job is to get as much money out of you as possible. They work for the manufacturers, not you. Their job is to convince you that you need everything that has ever been made! That is, to convince you that you're not cool, exciting, interesting, sexy, successful, or complete unless you have that one specific product that they're advertising!

Think about it: you can't drive down a road, open a magazine or newspaper, or switch on the TV or the radio without being told of all the things you can't live without, who moments ago you didn't even know existed! The impact of advertisers on the "free world" is enormous. They try to tell you what you should look like, how you should act, and who you should be. Buy now, pay later—you're worth it.

I cringe every time I hear that line, one of their favorites: "You're worth it." Well, you certainly are worth it to them! In fact, you're worth millions to them, if they can just get you to buy more stuff. Advertisers are masters at human psychology. They know that one of the most powerful drivers is human connection, that people want to be liked and to feel that they belong. I recommend that you read Robert Cialdini's book *The Power of Persuasion* to really understand what's happening in the world to help relieve you of your money.

Don't get me wrong: I love "nice things." Dave and I have lots of toys that we really enjoy. I'm not advising you to be a penny-pinching miser and to lower your standard of living. That isn't wealth. In fact, it's the opposite. I simply want you to increase your standard of living by being financially free.

Credit cards, overdrafts, revolving credit

The objective of banks and other lending institutions is to make as much profit as they legally can. There is absolutely nothing wrong with any business making a profit—in fact, they must. I myself love profit, but I don't get confused as to whose interest banks and lenders are looking after! The primary aim of the lending industry is to separate you from as much of your money as possible, and they accomplish this by charging their customers high interest rates and plenty of fees.

Banks and other lenders want the power. They want you to be a slave to your debt for as long as possible, preferably until you die, and then they'll get a little more from any estate you may have managed to accumulate.

Credit cards are deliberately designed with very small minimum monthly payments, so that you never pay them off. The lender wants you to pay interest for as long as possible and so he keeps encouraging you to put just a little bit more on the plastic. In fact, he'll offer you a higher credit limit, special offers, and incentives to spend just that little bit more—incentives such as loyalty programs, which usually offer products and services you neither want nor need.

With most credit cards, if you only pay the minimum monthly payment, you'll end up spending close to four times more than what you would have actually paid for the original item. The average credit card takes 15 to 20 years to pay off, if you only make the minimum payment.

What about the car industry? Car manufacturers are actually in the lending business, not the car business! They build cars so they have a vehicle through which to lend money. The same happens in the home appliance and furnishing businesses. Lending is big business, and everyone wants a piece of the pie—your pie!

Let's look at the word "mortgage" now—which comes from the French word *mourir*: to die. It is meant to be a debt until death . . . if that isn't slavery, I don't know what is!

A mortgage places a huge burden on a family: most people are usually advised to take out a 20-year mortgage and, what's more, the sales person at the bank will kindly help you get the maximum mortgage you can, over the longest period possible!

The reason for this, ostensibly, is smaller payments. The mortgage sales person advises this because they know full well that a typical family moves, on average, every seven years, and the biggest profits for the lenders are in the first few years of the mortgage, when almost all the monies paid in go toward paying interest and very little toward reducing the principal.

In fact, in the early years, more than 97 percent of what you pay is pure interest! What's more, most people sell their house only to go and buy a larger one with a new, bigger 20-year mortgage, thus starting the whole process all over again! When you consider that the average person moves into a new house every seven years without fully paying off the mortgage on the old one, you can see how someone can be on their 20th year of home ownership and still owe 92 percent on their mortgage!

But yes, you can turn these "deathly" amortizing schedules in your favor! Choose to pay off your mortgage quicker, thereby paying off more of your principal, rather than just the interest. This will save you thousands and also free up thousands more to buy more Assets.

Freeze it up!

If you currently have consumer debt, stop using any credit cards and get used to living off your Necessity Pot, using only cash or a debit card.

"But what about emergencies, Ann. Surely I'm going to need something for those?" I hear you ask. Don't worry, these can be covered, and here's how.

Keep one (just one!) low-fee credit card on hand for emergencies only. DO NOT KEEP THIS CARD IN YOUR WALLET. Otherwise, you'll try to convince yourself that a tub of Ben and Jerry's ice cream is an "emergency." Take the card and place it inside a metal can filled with water. Freeze it, as it will take several hours to defrost—giving you time to decide if the purchase is really an emergency and, therefore, "defrost-worthy."

My niece Cal took this advice and was really glad she had the extra time to think things through before she splurged: she and her boyfriend had accepted an invitation to a "free lunch," which was in fact a holiday club/time-share promotion.

They got swept away with all the slick sales talk and the very "sensible" persuasive arguments of all the future money that they would save on holidays if they signed up for the time-share points system. In addition, if they signed up on the spot and paid a deposit with their credit card that very same day, they'd get even more benefits! Very excitedly, they both signed up, but obviously didn't have the card on them.

They dashed home, full of excitement, to get the card out of the freezer, putting it out to thaw, so that they could seal the "special" deal before the end of the day. Its being in a metal tin, however, meant that Cal couldn't defrost it in the microwave—very clever! Over the course of the four hours that it took for the credit card to defrost, doubts about the purchase started to sink in. The defrost period is a period to let go of the emotions of a purchase and evaluate it in the context of your bigger goals. Cal also decided to call me and get another opinion on this so-called great deal.

Before the card had defrosted, Cal and her boyfriend had come to their senses: she'd refocused on her primary goal of buying her first property and had canceled the deal.

I'm so proud of her. Three years later, she is the owner of not one but two investment properties, has paid off her student loans, has absolutely no consumer debt whatsoever, and is continuing on her journey to financial freedom very quickly. Not bad for a 29-year-old!

Her credit card is still in its tin in the freezer.

Understanding the forces at play and how you—along with 95 percent of the population!—got yourself into debt, means that you can now use this awareness and change your outcome. Here's how.

The Debt Destroyer Recipe

- Step 1 -
Stop using the cards!

There's no way round this step, in many respects perhaps the most essential component of the Debt Destroyer Recipe: stop using your credit cards! If you can't pay cash for something, then you don't need it.

If you feel resistance coming up to this statement and still think you need stuff you can't afford, I recommend you reevaluate what's really important in your life: stuff or freedom?

When, and only when, you've paid off all your consumer debt and have mastered the money management recipes of a successful Wealth Chef, then, and only then, should you consider using a credit card again. And even then, you'll only be using it the smart way—that is, paying off your balance in full every month.

I'm not recommending that you literally pay cash for everything—you can pay with a debit card. Debit cards won't allow you to spend more than you have available and most banks also let you download your debit card transactions electronically via online banking, so you also have a very easy and manageable way to track and see exactly just where your money went.

So cut those credit cards up! Cut them all up, except the one sitting in its can in the freezer.

If you're now thinking, "I don't need to cut them up! I just won't use them anymore," then please be aware that you're just kidding yourself!

Would you, for example:

- Go on a diet but keep a chocolate bar in your pantry?

- Quit drinking but have a glass of wine at a party?

- Stop smoking but carry a pack of cigarettes in your pocket?

The answer is: no, you would not! Not if you were serious about changing your life. And if you're serious about getting out of debt and building wealth, then you have to take some serious action.

But don't get depressed about this. Turn it into a party! Have a retirement ceremony for your credit cards: gather your family together and share your vision for the future. Tell stories of the dumbest things you've ever bought with a credit card. Get out the scissors and start snipping! Celebrate the fact that you are no longer at the mercy of the credit companies. You're taking back your power!

I say cut them up, *but* don't cancel the credit card account! This is extremely important—don't cancel any accounts, not even the accounts you owe nothing on. This has to do with your credit rating (we'll get to it later on in more detail), but for now, cut up your cards and keep the accounts open.

- Step 2 -
Debt destroyer fuel

To destroy your debt, you need to pour fuel onto your debt pile. And to do this, you need Debt Destroyer Fuel (DDF).

DDF is the extra money you'll be adding to your regular monthly payments to accelerate your debt payoff. DDF is the key ingredient in the whole Debt Destroyer Recipe, and so it's vital that you do whatever it takes to make this as large as possible.

Aim to make your DDF equal to 10 percent of your Income. Now that you're a master at slicing and dicing, you're going to take this 10 percent from the following pots: 5 percent from your long-term savings pot and 5 percent from your giving pot.

If that just made you turn pale, don't panic! That's your target. For now, just start with whatever amount you can. But remember: destroying your debt is the most important thing in your life right now, so go through your Expenditure and see what you're prepared to cut out for a while, in order to add this fuel to your debt destruction.

As you pay off your debts, the amount of extra money you have to add to your DDF will increase, and by the time all your debt is paid off, you'll have at least 10 percent of your Income to invest, in addition to your investment pot.

- Step 3 -
See the whole picture!

Truth time! Gather together all your debts into one pile. This includes all your credit card balances, student loans, car loans, store card balances, mortgage, and so on. If your money management system has been a little on the chaotic side and you don't know how much you still owe on various debts, just call the lender and determine exactly what's owed.

And if you haven't done so already, download the Debt Destroyer Recipe and the Debt Destroyer Spreadsheet from The Wealth Chef webpage.

Now, using the Debt Destroyer Recipe Card and the examples given here, you're going to complete your Debt Destroyer Planner.

First, transfer the details of the debts to the Debt Destroyer Priority Planner spreadsheet. On this spreadsheet, you'll have one line for each of your debts, followed by eight columns.

For each debt, write down the following in the first four columns:

1. Who you owe the money to

2. The total outstanding balance—that is, what you still owe

3. The current interest rate you're being charged

4. The minimum monthly payment

Add up the total of columns two and columns four. (The spreadsheet will do this for you automatically.) This will show you how much total debt you have to pay off, as well as the total amount you need to pay in minimum monthly payments.

- Step 4 -
Debt priority ratio

Now, calculate the debt priority ratio. This is done by dividing the total outstanding balance by the minimum monthly payment. We're going to use it to determine the order in which you're going to destroy your debt. The answer goes into column five (and, once again, the spreadsheet will do this for you).

- Step 5 -
Debt destruction priority
Sweep One

Using the Snowball Debt Destruction Method, the first debt to be eliminated is the one that takes the least time. This is to boost you emotionally and, in addition, it will help you stick to the plan: in column six, you'll now be prioritizing your debts, which will tell you which debt you're going to destroy first.

- DEBT DESTROYER PRIORITY PLANNER -

Balance Start Date

	1	2	3	4	5	6	7	8	9
	Debt Name	Total Debt Amount Outstanding	Interest Rate	Minimum Monthly Payment	Debt Priority Ratio	Debt Destruction Priority	Detest You Most Factor 1 - 10	Months to Pay Off with Minimum Payment Only	Interest Paid
	Who you owe	Outstanding balance	Fill in from your statement	Fill in from your statement	Column 2/ Column 4	Lowest debt ratio in Column 5 is priority 1, and so on	1 = lowest DYM, 10 = highest DYM		
1	Acme Credit Card	$2,800	18%	82	34	2	9	70	$2,940
2	Bank Overdraft	6,500	21%	210	31	1	10	68	7,682
3	Car Loan	11,350	9%	165	69	3	8	142	12,096
4	Student Loan	24,000	4.5%	215	112	4	7	192	17,280
5	Mortgage	172,000	3.5%	1,150	150	5	5	265	133,090
	TOTAL	216,650		1,822				265	173,088
	TOTAL, Excluding Mortgage	20,650		457				192	39,993
	Years to pay off without the Debt Destroyer Recipe, including mortgage							22	
	Years to pay off without the Debt Destroyer Recipe, excluding mortgage							16	
	SORT THE TABLE ABOVE BY COLUMN 6 ASCENDING so that your priority 1 debt is listed first								
	Debt Destroyer Fuel (DDF)	10% of monthly Income *		£80		*5% from savings + 5% giving			

Start with the lowest debt priority payoff ration number in column five: find the lowest number in this column and put a 1 in column six. Now find the next lowest number and put a 2 in column six. Continue with all your debts in this way, until each debt has a debt destruction priority.

Now sort the rows of debt in your Debt Destroyer Planner so that the priority debt is in the first row.

- Step 6 -
Debt destruction priority
Sweep Two

Up until now we've applied logic and sense to the debt destruction recipe. But as we all know, debt isn't logical. What's logical about going out and buying a whole load of stuff you don't really need, with money you don't have? What's logical about taking years to pay four times more for something than it actually cost in the first place, for an item you most probably aren't even using anymore?

If we try to use only logical methods to destroy something that isn't logical, they just won't work.

The magical secret ingredient in this incredibly powerful Debt Destroyer Recipe, the one that will make your debt destruction plan totally irresistible, is the Detester Element.

This is the key and final step in determining the debt destruction priority listing in your Debt Destroyer Recipe, and the one that makes all the difference, creating a hunger in you to destroy your debt, far more powerful than the hunger to spend money that you don't have!

Now that you know which debt should be paid off first, using the Debt Snowball, you're going to add your own totally illogical, but very powerful DYM—Detest You Most—factor.

Go through every debt you have, line by line, and think about what you spent the money on that resulted in this particular debt, and then think about what this debt is preventing you from doing, having, and being.

Think about what you're having to drag around with you until this debt is destroyed and you can finally let it go and leave it in your past.

Once you've done that and are really feeling what each debt is preventing you from having, being, and doing, apply your DYM factor each debt. Add a number between 1 and 10, 10 being "I detest you the most," in column seven.

Based on your very powerful emotions, this will tell you which debt you need to focus on first: if your highest DYM factor is on the debt you identified as debt priority one in step five—great, you've confirmed that this is the debt that you're going to destroy first. If not, see which debt has the highest DYM factor against it and change this to your debt destruction priority one position, then renumber the rest of your debts accordingly in column six.

Awesome! You now have a very clear list of all your debts, how much you owe, your monthly minimum payments, and the exact order in which you're going to destroy them!

- Step 7 -
Destroy your debts!

We've arrived at the most exciting part of the Debt Destroyer Recipe: you're about to witness, with your own eyes, that, by following this recipe, it really is possible to become completely debt free within four to seven years.

You'll be continuing to pay the minimum payment on every debt, while accelerating the repayment on your top priority debt (the minimum payment + the Debt Destroyer Fuel amount).

When Priority Debt 1 is repaid, you continue paying the minimum on all the other debts, while priority Debt 2 is destroyed with its minimum payment + DDF + minimum payment from Debt 1.

Can you see now how the debt repayment amount starts to build up, like a gigantic snowball, wiping out your debt, faster and faster? Continue with this until every debt is a thing of the past.

- DEBT DESTROYER PRIORITY PLANNER - Prioritized -

Balance Start Date

	1	2	3	4	5	6	7	8	9
	Debt Name	Total Debt Amount Outstanding	Interest Rate	Minimum Monthly Payment	Debt Priority Ratio	Debt Destruction Priority	Detest You Most Factor 1 - 10	Months to Pay Off with Minimum Payment Only	Interest Paid
	Who you owe	Outstanding balance	Fill in from your statement	Fil in from your statement	Column 2/ Column 4	Lowest debt ratio in Column 5 is priority 1, and so on	1 = lowest DYM, 10 = highest DYM		
2	Bank Overdraft	$6,500	21%	$210	31	1	10	68	$7,682
1	Acme Credit Card	2,800	18%	82	34	2	9	70	2,940
3	Car Loan	11,350	9%	165	69	3	8	142	12,096
4	Student Loan	24,000	4.5%	215	112	4	7	192	17,280
5	Mortgage	172,000	3.5%	1,150	150	5	5	265	133,090
	TOTAL	216,650		1,822				265	173,088
	TOTAL, Excluding Mortgage	20,650		457				192	39,998
	Years to pay off without the Debt Destroyer Recipe, including mortgage							22	
	Years to pay off without the Debt Destroyer Recipe, excluding mortgage							16	
	SORT THE TABLE ABOVE BY COLUMN 6 ASCENDING so that your priority 1 debt is listed first								
	Debt Destroyer Fuel (DDF)	10% of monthly Income *		560		*5% from savings + 5% giving			

- DEBT DESTROYER PLAN -			
	Priority Monthly Payment = DDF + Cumulative Min. Payment	Months to Pay Debt with DDF	Interest Paid
Priority Debt 1 monthly payment	$790	8	$936
Priority Debt 2 payment, once Priority Debt 1 is destroyed	872	2.4	448
Priority Debt 3 payment, once Priority Debt 2 is destroyed	1,037	9.2	1,695
Student Loan payment, once Priority Debt 3 is destroyed	1,252	16	3,210
Mortgage Payment, once Priority Debt 4 is destroyed	2,402	54.5	45,248
Total Months to destroy Consumer Debt		36	
Total Years to destroy Consumer Debt		3	
Interest Paid on Consumer Debt with DDF			6,289
Interest Saved on Consumer Debt			33,709
Total Months, including mortgage		90	
Total Years to destroy all debt, including Mortgage		7.5	
Interest Paid on all debt with DDF			51,537
Interest Saved			121,551

- Step 8 -
Stick to your plan and focus on your wealth

WARNING: As you start seeing your debt destroyed, please be very aware of any diminishing in your desire to be debt free!

You see, for many people it's more important to be "not poor" than it is to be wealthy. If this is the case for you, you may feel the pressure to be debt free lifting once a few debts are destroyed, and be tempted to ease off the pace and even perhaps spend a little on credit. Maybe you just want to reward yourself with a holiday for how far you've come and you may believe that it's no problem if you put it on the credit card—after all, you've learned how to destroy it!

Trust me: if you fall for this temptation, you'll cause serious damage, not only to your debt destruction but to your whole wealth journey! Why?

Because you will have told yourself you don't have what it takes and will start believing this! Therefore, please be aware of this possibility and commit to staying the full course!

Most people pay off all of their credit cards within one year, and their car and student loans by the second year. By the third year, all of the money goes to pay off their mortgage. With the money they've saved from having no credit card or other loans, most people are able to double their mortgage payments. Within four to seven years, most people are able to pay off their mortgages and be completely DEBT FREE! Imagine that.

Susan's Story

You can see from the example sheets above the huge impact the Debt Destroyer Recipe has on the time it will take you to destroy your debts and the interest you'll pay.

The following is a real-life example from one of my private clients—Susan.

Without the Debt Destroyer Recipe, Susan was going to pay a staggering $40,000 in interest on her consumer debts and over $173,000 in interest, with her mortgage included. In addition, it was going to take her 16 years to pay off her consumer debt if she kept paying off only the minimum monthly payment—22 years, including her mortgage. Talk about depressing!

Susan decided to change her debt story and implemented the Debt Destroyer Recipe. She ordered her debts in terms of priority and determined the debt pay-off ratio and the debt pay-off priority. She was happy with the pay-off priority but when she applied the DYM factor, she realized that she hated her bank overdraft the most and so that became her first debt to destroy.

Susan committed to fueling her debt destruction with $580, in addition to the minimum monthly payments, and this was applied to her bank overdraft first.

As you can see in the example sheet, Susan was able to pay off all her consumer debt in just three years, saving a huge $33,700 in interest, and she then paid off her mortgage in a further 4.5 years, saving a total $121,500 in interest!

Instead of paying others this money, Susan was able to put that money into her own Wealth Pots and accelerate her journey to financial freedom exponentially. That is the impact of this powerful recipe.

Congratulations, you've now learned the Debt Destroyer Recipe!

Earlier, I mentioned not canceling your cards just yet because of your credit score, your Wealth Health Certificate. One of the factors the credit score companies use to assess your wealth health is your ratio of debt to the amount of credit you have available. As you clear your debt, you'll be improving this ratio, but only if you keep the underlying available credit in place. With time, you must cancel some of the available credit if there's a lot of it, but do so in a structured and conscious manner.

So that's it! Put your Debt Destroyer Plan in place now and make your payments as automatic as possible. Stick to the plan and focus on your wealth.

Focus on expanding your Income and your Asset Drawer. Yes, I'm going to say it again: energy flows where focus goes, and things that have energy flowing to them expand, like sunshine on a veggie garden—so make sure your energy is flowing to the things you want to expand in your life, such as love, success, wealth, and health. And keep on going!

Blitz That Debt!

LEVEL OF DIFFICULTY > Easy

. . . .

INGREDIENTS:

- 5 percent from "Savings Pot"
- 5 percent from "Contributions Pot"
- All your debts = everything you owe
- Debt Destroyer Fuel (DDF)
- Freezer in which to put your cards on ice

SKILLS REQUIRED:

- Determination
- Spreadsheets: a tiny amount

TIME REQUIRED:

- 3 hours initial setup
- 10 minutes per month, to adjust DDF

TOOLS REQUIRED:

- Balance Sheet: your Liabilities

METHOD:

. . . .

Step 1 > Stop Using the Cards.

Put an emergency card in the freezer. Do not cancel the rest yet.

Step 2 > Determine your DDF amount.

Commit to a fixed amount of money that you're going to use to destroy your debt.

Aim to make your DDF 10% of your Income: 5% from your Savings Pot and 5% from your Contributions Pot.

Step 3 > Get the Whole Picture.

Fill in the Debt Destroyer Priority Planner spreadsheet with every single debt you have, stating:

> a. Who you owe
> b. The total outstanding balance

Cont. >

    c. The current interest rate
    d. The minimum monthly payment

Step 4 > Determine the Debt Priority Ratio.

Divide the outstanding balance by the minimum monthly payment to get the debt priority ratio.

Step 5 > Debt Destruction Priority Sweep 1.

Sort your debt by priority with the lowest priority ration number being the highest priority debt.

Step 6 > Debt Destruction Priority Sweep 2—Detester Element.

Go through every debt and determine which debt you DETEST the most. Add a number between 1 and 10, a 10 being "I detest you the most."

Reorder your debt destruction priority by making the debt with the highest Detester number your number one priority debt.

Step 7 > Destroy Your Debts.

Pay the minimum payment on every debt and accelerate the repayment on your number one priority debt with the minimum payment + the Debt Destroyer Fuel amount.

When Priority Debt 1 is repaid, continue paying the minimum on all other debts, while Priority Debt 2 is destroyed with its minimum payment + DDF + minimum payment from Debt 1.

Continue until all your debts are destroyed.

Step 8 > Stick with your plan and watch your debt disappear.

. . . .

Breathe, Relax, and Focus
on expanding you and your investments,
knowing your debts are a thing of the past

13.

Wealth Recipe #4: Protection Pâté

You've already learned and implemented three of the five core Wealth Recipes. With this fourth recipe, you'll be well on your way to achieving financial freedom.

You now:

- Understand Wealth Flows and have in place your very own Wealth Cooking measures: your Balance Sheet and your Income Statement.

- Know what it is you are creating, and most important, why.

- Know exactly where you are in terms of your wealth journey, as well as the precise results you need in order to become financially free.

- Know exactly how big your Financial Freedom Feast needs to be, so that it can feed you for life.

- Have a very clear seven-course menu to divide the feast into bite-size, achievable dishes that you can focus on and measure your progress against.

- Understand the difference between an Asset and a Liability!

- Are carving up your pie in a way that expands your dough, gets your money working for you, and destroys your debt.

Wow!

Give yourself a huge pat on the back and let's get our sleeves rolled up for the last recipe, in which we'll be covering a subject most people would rather not discuss: death.

If money is a topic that most people would rather avoid talking about, then discussions about death, disability, not being able to earn an Income because of an accident, or your family being left destitute because you've either died or can't earn an Income are not exactly most people's favorite conversations, either!

Well, luckily, you're not just reading this book for a pleasant dinner-party conversation: we're here together to get your money supporting and working for you—so that you can sleep that much easier at night.

You also agreed to shine a light into dark places, face your fears, and do something about it! So, please keep your flashlight on high beam because I'm going to show you that all this stuff isn't actually all that complicated or even terribly scary.

Cause and effect

Listen to most people who are living a life they're not enjoying:

- "I'm overweight because . . . I've got a thyroid problem."
- "I'm poor because . . . I come from a poor family."
- "I don't manage my money well because . . . I'm bad at math."

They're living on the effects side of things. If you choose the easy path, this is where you are. You give away your personal power: you make someone or something responsible for your feelings, not you—hence, it is they or the thing that need to change, not you. You come to think that you will always be poor until you manage to not come from a poor family. Talk about being doomed!

Can you see the trap?

Most people try to change the event. But this is outside of ourselves and something over which we have no control. More often than not, the event is in the past—so these people are doomed because we can't change the past! When people make excuses, the cause is placed wrongly outside of themselves.

Let's look at the following statement: "I'm bulimic because I was abused as a child." If this were true, it would mean that I will always be bulimic . . . until I am no longer one who was abused as a child! You cannot escape; this is what this means—and I don't know about you, but I don't like it!

Now, let's see the difference if you choose to live on the cause side of things.

"Because I was abused as a child, I . . ."

Wow—notice the difference, notice how instead of closing down options, a tiny shift to the other side of cause, results in an infinite number of possibilities opening up. And how about the following statement?

"Because I grew up in a poor family, I . . ." Infinite possibilities.

The cause side of things is a place of power, movement, solution, and creativity. It's the place when you decide to take ownership of your own destiny. If you choose to stay on the effects side, how many options do you have? None! If you choose to live on the cause side, how many options do you have? An infinite number!

The cause side is not always a rose garden, but it's a powerful place, a place of personal power. It offers a challenge: believing that everything you need is already within you, and finding a way to create the life you desire.

"I'm a wonderful, gorgeous, creative, and wealthy being choosing to live at 'cause' and taking responsibility for all the results in my life." Say this to yourself, over and over again, if you choose to live on the cause side.

And read this chapter: it's about looking at the what-if scenarios and choosing to minimize their potential impact on you, those you love, and your finances.

This entire book is about putting in place the strongest foundation you can, to enable you to launch yourself to financial freedom. It's also about personal responsibility and taking back your power to control your destiny and live the life you choose to live. There are, however, some things we just cannot control—but we can be prepared, if they do occur, so that we can minimize their impact. I'm talking about illness, death, and natural disasters.

Preparing for things we just cannot control

All that's required is a little clearheaded thinking and the courage to have a few difficult conversations with your loved ones and yourself.

"What? More tough conversations, Ann?" you may be thinking. As always, I'll do my best to make the whole process as painless as possible, but before we go any further, I'm going to ask you a few questions. Please answer honestly:

- **If a disaster happened and your home was destroyed** by a flood, fire, or major storm, do you have the necessary insurances in place to replace everything you lose?

- **If you had an accident or fell ill** and were not able to bring in your usual Income for a period of time, do you have Income protection in place to supplement the Income until you're able to earn again? (This is to avoid having to consume your Financial Freedom Feast before it's ready to support you or, worse, losing your home because you can't pay the bills.)

- **If you were to become very ill and couldn't speak for yourself,** do you have the paperwork in place that would allow the person of your choosing to make urgent decisions regarding your health and medical care?

- **If you were to become incapacitated,** do you have the paperwork in place that allows the person of your choosing to handle your financial affairs?

- **If you were in the hospital on life support,** do you have the paperwork in place to allow the person of your choosing to communicate your wishes to the doctor?

- **If you were to die tomorrow,** are your dependents protected? Do you have everything in place so that the adult of your choosing can handle the financial aspects of their care in the manner you desire? Do you have insurances in place that will make sure they're not financially devastated as a result of losing you?

- **Do you have in place—right now—a will** defining how your Assets should be managed and what goes to whom? Is your will structured to minimize inheritance tax so that your loved ones get your feast and not the tax man?

If you answered "yes" to all these questions, then rock and roll! Your Protection Pâté ingredients are already in your life. However, please still read this chapter carefully, so that you can review what you have in place, to make sure it's appropriate.

If you answered "no" to any of these questions, then this chapter most definitely deserves your close attention!

And if you answered "no" to all of them, then please remember: you don't know what you don't know—most people are just never taught this stuff, so (let's say this together!) "No shame, no blame!" No need to beat yourself up!

Protecting yourself

This is all about protecting yourself, what you have, and those who depend on you financially. Just as you need the fridge and freezer in your kitchen that you use to preserve and keep your ingredients fresh, so you need to have appliances in your Wealth Kitchen that will keep you, your family, and your Assets safe and protected.

In the preceding chapters, you learned how to take charge of your financial life, destroy your debt, and create wealth by filling up your Asset Drawer. Now it's time to learn how to protect it all.

Being a Wealth Chef is about being prepared for any eventuality and about being realistic about the risks out there. There are some acts of nature that are beyond your control and you need to take action to protect yourself.

First, there are a set of must-have documents and insurances that are a key part of your protection: wills, Living Trusts, enduring powers of attorney, Living Wills, and insurances. Not the most fun topic to be discussing, as I mentioned before, but vitally important! You must know exactly what documents you need to keep in your Wealth Kitchen and the types of insurance—life, home, car, disability, and critical health—you should have and, equally important, shouldn't have. You must know the amount of coverage you need and how to buy it cost-effectively.

Your key wealth documents

The first one is a will. A will spells out how you want your Assets and certain possessions to be passed on to your loved ones after you die. It states who inherits what.

A properly structured will also ensures your loved ones get as much of your estate as possible, and that it doesn't all end up with the tax man!

Having a will is vitally important for a number of reasons: it goes a long way to preempting any disputes among your heirs, it ensures that your estate gets distributed among your beneficiaries in the way you wish, and it can also specify who you want to become the legal guardians of your children, in the event of both parents dying.

If you die without a will, you die intestate—this is the term given to the act of dying without a legal will. To have died "in intestacy" means a court-appointed executor will compile any Assets of the deceased, pay any Liabilities, and distribute the Assets to those parties deemed as beneficiaries. In plain English, if you die without a will, your estate gets divided up and distributed according to a fixed set of laws (which depend on where you live) by a probate court and a court-appointed executor.

Not only will this division not be how you want it to be, it also takes an exceptionally long time, costs a great deal of money, and ensures that the tax man gets most of it. While the court is getting around to sorting out your estate, those you love and who may depend on your estate to survive may not be able to access any of the money. The process can take years.

The bottom line is you do not want to die intestate. Put a will in place now!

Key points to bear in mind when making your will:

- You must nominate an executor of your estate—this person will handle the administration of your estate.

- You should keep your will as clear and simple as possible.

- You must update your will regularly, and especially in the event of divorce or death of a spouse or a beneficiary.

A will is your first vital wealth document to have on your Wealth Kitchen shelf and part of your Protection Pâté. Those whom you want to manage or be the executors of your estate will need to know where you keep it. So do remember to first tell them they've been named as executors and, second, where you keep all your important financial documents!

A will, however, only addresses matters once you die. It doesn't deal with what happens if you become incapacitated. You should also consider having a Living Trust. This isn't available in every country, and so I won't go into detail about it here, but I encourage you to research it in your own country.

A Living Trust is a way to minimize the taxes that will be triggered on your Assets when you die, in both the form of capital gains and estate duty. You can also include an incapacity clause in a Living Trust, specifying a person who will handle your financial affairs in the event of your not being able to, due to some form of diminished capacity—an illness or an accident.

If you don't have a Living Trust, you'll need an Enduring Power of Attorney that specifically nominates a person to handle your financial affairs, and gives this person all the powers to do so, if you're not able to, once again, because of some form of diminished capability. If you've had an accident and are in the hospital, unable to talk or sign documents, then the Enduring Power of Attorney document gives someone you trust all the powers necessary to manage your finances.

The final document I believe you need in your Wealth Kitchen is an Advance Directive for health care. This is also known as a Living Will. I know this isn't stuff we choose to think about and it's also pretty hard to even imagine a time when we may be physically incapable of speaking for ourselves. (I know Dave can't imagine any scenario where I wouldn't be able to make myself heard.) This is one of the toughest subjects I want you to consider, but I know firsthand how important it is. If I chose to avoid it, then I wouldn't be serving you.

My mother fell ill, and in a matter of days she was on life-support and unable to communicate. As the family gathered round, we had to have the discussion about what my mom would have wanted. Would she want to be kept on life support for an indefinite period. Would she want to be revived if there was a chance of then living in a significantly diminished capacity? These were questions we asked ourselves, and were asked. Fortunately, our mother had written a Living Will. In the document, she stated very clearly what her wishes were, in just such an event.

Not only did this document ensure that her wishes were known and met when she couldn't talk for herself, but it also meant we didn't have to decide for her. Even though we all believed we knew what she wanted, as we'd discussed it as a family, without the Living Will document we would have had to go to court to have her wishes met—which would have been expensive, have dragged on for days and months, and also have been emotionally devastating in what was already a very difficult time.

So I really encourage you to face this subject head-on and create a single document that expresses your wishes and gives you the security of knowing you've protected yourself and your loved ones in a worst-case scenario.

The first part of the document, the Advanced Directive, spells out the level of medical intervention you want in the event that you can't speak for yourself. There are numerous templates and societies in most countries that will assist you with this and explain the various levels and options.

A lot of personal development tells us to focus on the things we want in our lives—I support this philosophy and I've also referred to it frequently throughout this book: energy flows where focus goes. So, you may be asking, "Why are we then focusing on things we don't want, such as sickness, dying, and all that stuff?"

I believe true wealth and personal accountability and responsibility come from being able to look at the worst-case scenarios, to be reconciled with them, to have put in place all you can to minimize and manage the risks—and then, with that done, to look toward the things that you want in your life, knowing that you have the dark parts securely dealt with.

Because, let's face it, ignoring something doesn't make it go away. In fact, pretending something doesn't exist often actually causes it to grow in our lives like the shadow of the "monster" created on the bedroom wall by that untrimmed hedge outside! When we simply switch a light on and go outside and have a good hard look at the monster—perhaps trimming a few bits here and there—the monster suddenly disappears and we can sleep soundly, dreaming of our financial feast and the glorious life we're living.

So, take a sip of water (or wine!), stand up and move your body, shake it all out, and give yourself a large, well-deserved pat on the back—congratulations! You've faced some pretty tough stuff square on, and I really commend you for that!

The five primary insurance categories

You've got your protection documents, and now you'll need some insurance products. These are the five primary insurance types which you must consider:

1. Life Insurance
2. Home Insurance
3. Car Insurance
4. Medical
5. Disability & Critical Health Insurance

Life insurance

Life insurance is important. If anyone in your life depends on your Income, be it your children, your spouse, or your parents, then you must protect them with a Life Insurance policy—until you have sufficient Assets in your Wealth Kitchen that can continue to feed them, even if you're not there.

When it comes to this subject, I typically find people fall into one of two camps: the Total Denials (which isn't a river in Egypt, as they later find out the hard way) who have no coverage and don't want to even talk about it. Then there's the other camp: the Chicken Littles, who've been filled with such fear and dread by financial advisers and insurance salesman that they have numerous Life Insurance policies, providing way more coverage than they need—and usually making the person who sold them more money than they're worth!

You need Life Insurance if anyone in your life relies on your Income. The question to ask is: "If I (or my partner/spouse) were to die today, would those I support be able to take care of themselves?" If the answer is no, then you need Life Insurance. And if that question made you squirm, work out what it is that you believe about your own mortality. Remember: taking responsibility for yourself and everything in your life is a fundamental characteristic to develop—and this includes being able to confront the risks in your life.

A special note for stay-at-home parents: just because you don't bring in an Income doesn't mean that you don't need Life Insurance! If you were to die, your partner or spouse would have to either hire someone else to look after the kids or stop working. This costs money and you need to ensure that the money is there if you aren't!

Now, having determined that you need Life Insurance, the question is: how long do you need it for? A Life Insurance broker (who is, essentially, a salesperson) will try to tell you that you need a top-of-the-range, hugely expensive Life Insurance policy that will cover you for your entire life. No way! You don't need whole Life Coverage and please don't fall for their fear tactics and smooth sales talk. Whole Life Coverage is the most hideous and insidious insurance product out there, and I can't think of anyone who would ever need it.

We're talking about *term* Life Coverage, meaning that it's Life Coverage for a period of time, or term. Life Insurance is supposed to provide financial protection for those dependent on you, up to the point when this is no longer the case and during the time you're building up your Assets.

Once you have sufficient Assets in your Wealth Pantry that can able to pay you a healthy Income that your dependents can fall back on if you were to die, you no longer need Life Insurance. In addition, those people dependent on you today will hopefully not be dependent on you in the future, so the size of the Assets and the size of the cover you need should shrink until you don't need it any longer.

Take my hubby and me: while we were building up our Asset Drawer, we both had Life Insurance policies in case either of us kicked the bucket. We have now reached a stage where our Asset Drawer is full enough for either of us to live on comfortably, should the other one die. We also have no other dependents, except our two cats and our dog, so we no longer have Life Insurance policies.

Most people need a term Life Insurance policy for no longer than 20 to 25. It will be even shorter if you master and apply all the Wealth Recipes, because you'll build up your Asset Drawer to a sufficient size well before that. My suggestion to you is to put your term Life Insurance policy in place for just a few years longer than the time it will take you to create your Financial Freedom Feast. Remember, never a whole life!

Next, let's work out how much insurance you'll need.

Before we proceed, however, let's have a look at a few definitions:

Death Benefit: the money your beneficiaries receive upon your death. For example, a $5 million Life Insurance policy has a $5 million death benefit. Assuming the insured person dies while the policy is active (referred to as "in force" by the insurance industry), the beneficiaries of the policy will receive a $5 million payout. This is typically tax free.

Capital: this is the actual amount of the death-benefit payout.

Income: this is the interest/Income you can earn by investing the payout, the capital.

How big an insurance policy do you need?

So how big an insurance policy do you need? The answer is: one that is large enough, so that your beneficiaries can live off the Income/interest earned by the payout alone and not need to eat into the capital to survive.

How much you want that to be is totally up to you, but I suggest that, as a minimum, it's your current Rat Race Income amount that you identified in your Financial Freedom Feast menu. In this Menu, you also determined the Net Worth amount or lump sum you needed to produce that Income, which was based on an 8 percent interest rate.

Let's say you choose the $5 million death benefit. If you die, your beneficiaries will receive $5 million—which, if they choose to invest it, and invest it conservatively (at, say an 8 percent after-tax interest rate), they'd receive $33,333 a month to live on, without touching the capital amount.

This means that the next year, they'd continue to get $33,333 a month, and so on. If this amount per month is sufficient to cover your beneficiaries' expenses if you die, then a $5 million death benefit will be sufficient. But if they need, say, $50,000 a month to cover expenses, then they'd have to start eating into the capital amount to survive—which would, in turn, start reducing the future Income they'd get from the payout, resulting in their having to use up even more of the capital until, at some point, there would be nothing left.

This is why I recommend a term Life Insurance policy with a death benefit amount large enough for your dependents to survive on the Income/interest alone, indefinitely. By the way, I'm purposely using large amounts as examples, but remember that what you actually need is totally up to you to determine; it's your unique financial numbers that matter and nobody but you can determine what that amount is. So please don't let some financial product sales person tell you how big your term Life Insurance policy should be!

Even at your Rat Race Roast Income number you may be getting a bit pale at the size of the lump sum required. I know this might seem huge, but remember: it isn't for life! It's only for as long as you have dependents and don't have sufficient Assets in your wealth drawer.

Most Life Insurance salespersons will tell you that you only need five or six times your dependents' annual expenses. They're assuming that your dependents will adjust to a smaller Income and will find other ways to supplement the loss of your Income.

Well, I don't believe in the hope and chance school of wealth. Insurance is about preparing for the worst. What if one of your dependents was severely injured in the car accident that killed you and their Expenses go up, not down? Having an insurance policy that pays out sufficient for them to live on will give your surviving partner options to perhaps work only part time.

An 8 percent interest rate after tax is conservative and represents a lower risk/lower return investment. By using conservative interest rates, you're better covered for whatever the actual situation is—that is, much better than making projections on returns that may require a higher-risk investment. The trade-off for lower risk is a lower interest rate. And when it comes to looking after your dependents, we want as little risk as possible.

A death benefit payout of this size is an ideal goal and assumes you have no Assets in your Asset Drawer. If you can't manage the premium on a policy of this size, or you're still addressing your debt destruction, then you can scale back. In addition, if you've already built up a healthy Asset Drawer in your Wealth Pantry, you can reduce the death benefit payout proportionately. Also, if your dependents are older, you may choose a lower payout and consciously plan for them to use the capital amount.

The choice is yours

The choice is yours. But whatever you do, please make it a conscious choice based on knowledge and thought.

Many employers provide a Life Insurance policy as part of an employment package. This usually comes at no cost to you, but it is normally limited to between one and five times your annual pensionable Income. Make sure you know exactly what coverage your employer provides and then get a policy to cover the remaining amount.

Please bear in mind that topping up the Life Insurance policy provided by your employer is usually more expensive than an individual term life policy that you can get directly yourself. What's more, the "free" Life Insurance provided by your employer is only available while you work for them!

So make sure you check the coverage you get if you change to a new employer and ensure that the employer policy, together with your individual policy, always adds up to your desired death benefit payout.

You know now if you need Life Insurance, as well as for how long and how much. So what to buy? Most Life Insurance salespeople make hefty commissions by confusing people.

One of the "great" sales pitches they use is to try to convince you that Life Insurance is an investment. No, no, *no*! It is not an Asset; it is not an investment and it never will be, no matter how they try to dress it up.

You only ever want to buy a term Life Insurance policy—simple and straightforward, without any bells and whistles and definitely without any so-called investment component.

Never, under any circumstances, buy an endowment Life Insurance policy or a whole life one. Endowment policies are marketed as having the benefit of not only providing you with Life Insurance but also being an investment or savings vehicle. Don't fall for it. Endowment policies are fantastic for the sales person and disastrous for you. The sales person earns huge commissions from selling these policies, and you'll get almost nothing. If you already own an endowment-type policy, find out if it makes financial sense to get rid of it and replace it with a term Life Insurance policy. You may just need to accept the loss of the supposed savings you've already put into the policy. Remember: Wealth Chefs cut their losses and hold onto their wins!

Before comparing term Life Insurance policies, make sure you've worked out how long you'll need it for, as well as the amount of the death benefit payout. Stick to these and make sure that you're comparing apples with apples. The term and the death benefit payout will impact the cost of the insurance, as will your current age and health. The younger and healthier you are when you take out a term Life Insurance policy, the cheaper it will be.

When you ask for term Life Insurance quotes, ask for a fixed premium. This is also called "annual guaranteed renewable term," meaning that as long as you pay your premiums on time, they won't increase from year to year. Nor can the insurance company cancel your policy.

If you have an insurance agent you enjoy working with, then by all means work with him. But (and it's a big "but") please ensure he or she is independent and not working for a particular insurance company. You want them to shop around for the best policy for you and they can't do this if they're tied to a specific company. Get at least three term Life Insurance quotes and make sure you read all the small print!

When you buy your Life Insurance policy, you'll need to specify who your beneficiaries are—that is, who gets the payout if you die. This isn't as simple as it may sound. Think about what might happen if both you and your spouse or partner were to die in, say, a car accident, or if you're a single parent.

Insurance companies will not pay out policies to minor children (under 21), so don't make your minor children the beneficiaries. If you do this, the insurance company will require a guardian of the estate to be appointed, even if you've named a guardian in your will. This will cost your estate thousands and accessing the money can prove to be a nightmare, requiring court appearances every time your dependents need money.

Either nominate your chosen guardian as the beneficiary directly or put in place a revocable Living Trust that will be the beneficiary of your policy.

Please also ensure you keep your beneficiary information on all your policies up-to-date! I know a number of horror stories where people failed to update this information and when they died, their ex-husband or ex-wife got the payout and not their children, for whom the policy was intended!!

Life insurance shopping: six ways to save

1. Only ever buy term Life Insurance and then only for the lump sum amount you need to cover your dependents' living Expenses. When your Assets grow and your dependents diminish (your kids leave home someday . . . we hope!), you should reduce your Life Insurance coverage.

2. Don't add optional extras or any supposed savings components to your policy. Keep it simple!

3. Don't take up offers for small amounts of Life Insurance that you receive in the post or via e-mail: this kind of coverage is extremely expensive, compared to a single policy from a reputable insurer.

4. Quit smoking! Smokers pay up to 50 percent more on Life Insurance than nonsmokers.

5. Determine how much your employer can cover you for and only get a policy for the remaining death benefit needed.

6. Become an insurance surfer! Scour the Internet for reputable insurance companies and get a number of quotes before you seal the deal.

Home insurance

In my experience, most people are horribly under-insured when it comes to their Home Insurance and only discover this (with devastating consequences) when they need it most and discover that their payout won't cover a major loss.

If you own a home, you most probably have Home Insurance, and if you have a mortgage, you definitely will have it, as your lender will insist. I've discovered that many home owners have no idea what level of Home Insurance coverage they have and, in addition, it's usually inappropriate. You see, if your home is destroyed, you'll still be liable for the mortgage!

Pull out your Home Insurance policy (sometimes also called Building Insurance), as this insurance covers the fixed built parts of your home, not its contents. Review your policy and determine:

- How much will your policy pay if your home is destroyed?

- Does your coverage automatically increase every year to keep up with the increasing costs of construction?

- What coverage have you got in the event you can't live in your home due to damage?

- Does your policy include personal protection (Personal Liability Coverage) in the event you're sued?

The first point is the most important. This is what your insurer has agreed to pay if your home is damaged or destroyed and is called the "covered loss." There's a certain amount of confusion around this, in that many home owners don't fully understand that this insurance might not cover certain events. Go through the fine print and also call your insurance company and get them to tell you exactly what events are not covered. All telephone calls to an insurance company have to be recorded. These are kept on record. If, down the line, you need to make a claim for an event that the person on the phone told you was covered or didn't tell you wasn't covered and the insurance company tells you it's an uninsured event, you can go to the ombudsman and require that the telephone record be retrieved. (And if, in fact, the insurer didn't tell you that the event wasn't covered, you'll have a strong case!)

How much coverage do you need? Most people think about the market value of their home. Either what they paid when they bought it or what they believe they'd get if they were to sell it.

For home/building insurance, focus on the cost of rebuilding the house in the event of its being destroyed. This often works out to be more expensive than you may think.

Say you have a property with a market value of $400,000: it might take $300,000 to rebuild the house, meaning that your land value is $100,000. Generally speaking, you'll still have the land in the event of your home's being destroyed and so your Home Insurance needs to have a coverage of $300,000. When calculating your replacement costs, it's important to add the cost of your swimming pool (if you have one), paving, greenhouse, and so on.

If your policy states that you're covered for Actual Cash Value (ACV), then you're definitely underinsured. ACV means that your payout is based on the depreciated value of what needs to be replaced or repaired. Let's say your roof is ten years old and gets badly damaged in a big hail storm. The insurer will calculate your payout based on the value of a ten-year-old roof so as to restore the roof to the quality and value of one of that age.

Think about it: what good is that when you need to pay a roofer for a new roof? It will be you who will end up having to pay the difference between the ten-year-old roof value, and the actual cost of a new roof.

So if your Home Insurance policy coverage is based on ACV, call your insurance company now and change your policy to replacement cost.

Your Personal Liability Coverage is also very important. In the event of your being sued for accidentally hurting someone or damaging their property, Personal Liability Coverage helps pay for legal costs and damages. It also covers the cost of any injury caused by you, your family, or even your pets, on or off your property.

It's important to understand that if someone wins a judgment against you, they can go after your Assets. In this case, your home will be considered an Asset (even though, as a Wealth Chef, you know it isn't!). They'll also be able to get a judge to authorize impounding your salary, which means they'll get paid straight out of your salary check! Having Personal Liability Coverage protects your Assets and your salary from being seized.

Home contents insurance

Besides the actual structure of your home, you also need to insure your possessions in it. Most insurers use replacement value as the insured value of your home contents. Again, check your policy.

When determining the amount of coverage we need for home contents insurance, we usually think of how much the possessions cost us. That's great until you have a claim. Your insurer doesn't give a damn how much the items cost you, as they will calculate the cost of replacing the item now.

An assessor will come over to your home and add up the total replacement cost of everything in your home. They will then compare this total with the home contents insurance coverage amount you have in your policy. If the total replacement value, as calculated by the assessor, is more than your coverage, you will not be paid out the full replacement cost for the items that you're claiming. This is called the Insurance Averaging Ratio: it's the ratio of your insurance cover divided by the total current replacement value of your insured possessions. Your payout will be reduced by this ratio.

Now, here's the rub. If you're overinsured—that is, your coverage is more than the total current value of your insured possessions—you won't get paid out more! You will simply get the replacement value.

The bottom line is to make sure you know the current replacement value of *all* your insured possessions and ensure that your insurance policy coverage matches that amount. The best way to do this is to take an inventory of all your possessions. I know this may sound tedious, but it's one of those things you only have to do once, and then just update every year. It's also a good idea to take photos of specifically valuable items, art work and nonstandard furnishings, so that you have proof of the item, in the event of a claim.

Having this simple spreadsheet and a few photos stored in your filing system will make a significant difference in the event of your needing to make a claim.

If you have a large home with possessions of a high value, you may want to ask the insurance company to send out an assessor to do the inventory. These assessors are up to speed on current replacement values and will assess the replacement value of your possessions, in the same way that the insurance company will do in the event of a claim. For higher-value policies, insurance companies will often do this at no cost to you. Just ask.

Also take note of items such as jewelry, cameras, laptops, and expensive sports equipment. Your policy may require you to specify these items separately and you may need to pay for additional coverage to cover them outside of your home.

Note for renters: just because you're renting doesn't mean you don't need contents insurance! The landlord will have to have building insurance and he's responsible for damage to the physical structure but not the contents. If, say, a huge storm blows off the roof, the landlord will be responsible for replacing the roof, but if any of your possessions are damaged by flying debris or rain getting in, then the risk is your responsibility.

Also, make sure you have Personal Liability Coverage: if you accidentally burn down the property or cause damage to it, you'll be liable to pay for the damages and any injuries that may occur.

Home and contents insurance shopping

Wealth Chefs know and use a number of ways to reduce the costs of Home and Contents Insurance:

1. **Bundle your insurance policies together.** Get a quote for your home building, contents, and Car Insurance from the same company. This should bring your individual premiums down significantly. Just ensure you compare each component part of the total premium—that is, how much of the premium is for the building, how much for the cars, how much for content insurance. I review all my insurances annually and phone around for quotes to see if I can get a better deal. I always ask for bundled

quotes, and for each component to be individually specified. This way, I can let the numbers tell the story.

2. **Volunteer to pay an excess.** An excess is the amount of money you must pay for each insurable event, before the insurance kicks in. Choosing a higher excess can significantly reduce your premium. Remember, insurance is to cover you in the event of a major life event; it's not a savings plan or a nice toy to play with! Many people I know opt for a zero excess option on their insurance and then feel they should claim for every little thing they break or damage. This kind of thinking will come at a significant cost to you, as each claim you make will push your future premiums up, and, in extreme cases (if you make a lot of claims), you may become uninsurable with some companies. Choosing a higher excess also makes you more careful with your belongings and makes you really shop around to get the best prices for repairs or replacement. It helps you become more financially competent. What you're doing here, in effect, is self-insuring the first fixed amount of damage or loss. How? By having the money for it in your Security Soup Wealth Chef Pot. That way, the money stays with you if you don't need to use it. And you free even more money to invest, due to the lower premium you will be paying for insurance.

3. **Limit your claims.** Protect your no-claims bonus. Always calculate the value of the claim with the potential impact on your insurance premiums and the discount you get from your no-claims bonus. This can make a significant difference to your premium— as much as 25 to 45 percent per year.

4. **Find out if you are eligible for any discounts.** Such as those linked to having:
   - A security system installed in your home
   - Your home's being always occupied, especially if you work from home
   - Locks fixed to your windows
   - Fire extinguishers and smoke alarms
   - Being over 55 years old

   Often, the cost of installing these items pays for itself from the reduced insurance premium. And you get a safer home. It's a win all round.

5. **Find out if you're eligible to belong to schemes that apply to only certain groups of people.** Some insurance schemes are eligible only to, say, professional engineers. Because engineers are generally considered pretty conservative and typically make fewer claims than the general population, the whole scheme has lower premiums.

6. **Consider pay-by-the-month premium options.** Instead of paying an annual sum, consider these options, but first make sure that there's no additional cost for them. Ask for a quote with both an annual and

monthly payment option and work out the difference. Paying by the month allows you to manage your cash flow better.

7. **Avoid additional coverage options** and fancy add-ons unless they are genuinely free inclusions. These options are generally very poor value for you and typically include:
   - Coverage for spoilage in your fridge and freezer
   - Coverage for stolen credit cards
   - Pet coverage
   - Accidental breakage of glass
   - Appliance repair

8. **Surf for quotes.** Get a minimum of at least three quotes to compare and do this every year.

Car Insurance

It's compulsory to have third-party insurance to protect innocent victims of accidents from serious financial loss. In addition, it's advisable to top up this compulsory insurance with a policy designed to cover damage to other vehicles or property, as well as your own vehicle. Car Insurance is usually the biggest insurance cost you'll have, and I'll now show you how to reduce your premiums significantly.

First, let's understand the different insurance coverages:

- **Third-Party Injury.** This is the compulsory insurance already mentioned and is required before you can register a car. It covers both the car owner and the driver against any Liability in regard to death or injury to a person, caused by the fault of the car owner or driver. It does not cover damage to your car, other cars, or property.

- **Third-Party Damage.** If your car damages another person's property, and you are at fault, third-party property damage will cover these costs, as well as your legal costs. This coverage is recommended if your car is not worth replacing or repairing. If you have any Assets or intend to be stocking your Asset Drawer, then this insurance is what you need. Failure to cover your Liability of damage to other people's property puts your own Assets at serious risk.

- **Third-party, Fire and Theft.** As it says on the box, this type of insurance covers your car against fire damage or if it's stolen. It's usually an add-on to a third-party property damage policy. It does not cover your car in the event of a collision. This is, however, an unnecessary extra expense for something that only benefits you if your car is a total loss, but not as a result of an accident. In this case, comprehensive insurance is a better bet.

- **Comprehensive insurance.** This is the most common type of Car Insurance, covering all of the above and your own car in the event of an accident. If your car is financed, it's likely that your lender will insist on your having comprehensive insurance.

A key consideration when shopping for Car Insurance is the difference between agreed value and market value. Agreed value is where the insurer guarantees to pay you the amount nominated in your policy as the insured value of the vehicle, in the event of total loss. Market Value means that the amount nominated in your policy is the maximum that they will pay in the case of total loss.

The actual amount you get paid is very seldom the nominated market value, as the insurer will depreciate the value of the car and will only pay out the current market value of a replacement value car of a similar condition, often referred to as "the book value."

Agreed value is the best option if you own an unusual car. But with a standard vehicle, this policy is usually more expensive, so you need to weigh up the true value of the extra expense when making your decision.

Also bear in mind that the Agreed Value depreciates every year, so you need to keep an eye on this and remain vigilant as to whether the agreed value is realistic or not.

Ten ways to reduce the cost of your Car Insurance

Here they are:

1. **Consider the type of insurance you actually need.** Most people have comprehensive insurance, without considering whether it's really necessary.

Don't be emotional about your car. If the difference between your premium and the real value isn't too much, consider third-party property damage insurance and self-insure the additional risk. Put the difference in the premium into your Protection Pâté Wealth Pot, so you can cover any damage or loss of your car if you need to.

2. **Choose a voluntary excess.** Like building and contents insurance, opt for a high excess in order to keep your premiums low. I realize a low excess may give you a nice, warm, fuzzy feeling, but that feeling comes at a price! Low- or no-excess policies cost the insurance industry more than higher excess policies, because more claims are made against low- or no-excess policies and each small claim has an administration cost. A higher excess can save you as much as 30 percent on your premium.

3. **Never lodge small claims unless you're guaranteed they won't affect your no-claims bonus or your future premium increases.** Raise your excess and self-insure the small stuff.

4. **Put your premium savings into your Protection Pâté Wealth Pot.** While your premium savings are building up, keep your single low-or no-fee credit card in its tin in the freezer as your emergency fund. This will give you peace of mind, knowing that you can cover the excess costs if you need to.

5. **Sign up for an advanced and defensive driving course.** Many insurers will give you a discount for having been on this type of course, and you'll also have the benefit of being a better driver, one who is able to anticipate other drivers' mistakes. This reduces your risk of an accident significantly, giving you even more peace of mind about your higher excess option. Better yet, give yourself and your partner the advanced driving course as a birthday gift! Savings all round.

6. **Do not touch the fancy extras you're offered unless they are genuinely "free."** Emergency travel costs, car rental, cover for a handbag or laptop stolen from the car, and so on: these are hugely overcharged insurance items. Just say *no!* When the salesperson starts going on about all these wonderful extras, politely, but firmly, ask him for a quote without the extras!

7. **The best way to save on your insurance is to drive safely!** Protect your no-claims bonus! Remember, a drinking and driving conviction will significantly increase your insurance premium for a very long time. It's just not worth it.

8. **Consider the type of car you drive.** Conservative family cars will cost you significantly less to insure than high-powered sports cars. Adding market performance-boosting components to your car will also increase your insurance premiums. Check the insurance rating of the various cars you're considering when deciding which car to buy.

9. **Find out which discounts are available**. These may include:

   - Multicar policies or bundling with your home and contents insurance

   - Car not being used for business

   - Car being locked in a garage when parked at night and/or at your workplace

   - Antitheft devices and car tracking systems in the case of theft

   - Airbags

   - People over 55

   - Direct debit premiums paid monthly

   - Annual lump sum discount

10. **Be a quote surfer!** Shop around vigorously for quotes, and do so every year.

Medical Insurance

At some point in our lives we will all require some sort of medical assistance. But being a Wealth Chef is about being able to understand and select the right type and level of Medical Insurance you need, based on your lifestyle and situation.

You may be very privileged to live in a country with a very good national or public health system. If this is the case for you, respect it and add that to something to be very grateful for. However, even if you do, I still suggest you read the following, as most countries are finding their public health system less and less affordable and requiring private health coverage in some form to support it.

The main purpose of Medical Insurance, also called "medical aid," is to make sure you have coverage in the event of a major medical problem. You may find it more cost-effective to pay for routine medical services with your own money and rely on Medical Insurance only to protect you from a major event or catastrophe. You also need to consider your current life situation. Do you have young children who may require lots of doctors' visits, or are you older and have medical problems that require regular treatments?

Like all the other insurances that we've covered, you need to be unemotional and very realistic with what you actually need. If you're young, are healthy, and have no kids, I suggest you only need a hospital plan Medical Insurance policy. This is the cheapest policy, and you'll be covered in the event of any major medical event.

On the other hand, if you're a couple with young children and plan to have more, I recommend you shop around for fully comprehensive Medical Insurance.

The choice for medical aid has numerous variables and too many for me to cover here. Contact a good Medical Insurance broker, an independent one, who can advise you on options from a variety of different Medical Insurance companies, and then select the policy suitable for your current life situation.

Just remember: like all other insurance policies, don't get sucked into the special extras on offer, such as cheap gym memberships, free movie tickets, and so on. Focus on the Medical Insurance cover only when making your choice.

Income Protection, Disability, and Critical Illness Coverage

We're almost there! Well done for persevering this far! I know insurance isn't the sexiest topic, but understanding the role it plays in your Wealth Feast and being smart about protecting yourself and your Assets is what we do as Wealth Chefs.

Income Protection, Disability Coverage, and Critical Illness Coverage (sometimes also called "Dread Disease Coverage") are the last insurances I want you to consider.

If you're still dependent on the Income you get from your employment or active work, rather than the Income from your Asset Drawer, then you'll need to consider some form of Income Protection Insurance.

Income Protection Insurance provides you with a regular Income in the event you're unable to work in your normal employment, due to an accident or sickness. The benefit is usually paid monthly as Income, not as a lump sum, and is usually 75 percent of the Income that you insure.

A lot of employers provide an element of Income Protection, together with Life Insurance, so find out if you get any coverage from your employer first.

Remember: this insurance is to replace your Income if an unforeseen event prevents you from earning. It is not meant to pay for the associated costs of that event. That is what your Medical Insurance is for.

Insurance companies offer all sorts of confusing extras attached to their policies and may have a variety of different names for the products. Remember, you're looking for something to replace your Income only! Also be on the lookout for exclusions. Most Income Protection policies will refer to loss of Income due to sickness and accident. Just make sure of this!

In addition, review the definition of "total disability" in the policy. Some policies may require you to lose both legs, both arms, and both eyes before they will pay out! Other things to look out for are the types of duties or employment you must not be able to perform   in order to qualify for the payout. Some policies refer to "any employment," including low-paid, unskilled work totally unrelated to what you may currently be doing. So ensure your policy covers you for when you can't do your current regular work.

Critical Illness or Dread Disease Insurance pays out a lump sum benefit in the event you're diagnosed with one of a specified list of critical illnesses. This usually covers things such as cancer, heart attacks, strokes, etc. This is different from Life Insurance, in that it pays out when you are diagnosed with the illness and not when you die. This then enables the sick person to pay for the additional medical expenses they need, relieve financial pressure, and recover, without the added pressure of financial worries. As with other insurance policies, beware of exclusions and other conditions imposed.

A few points to consider

If you already have Medical Insurance, Life Insurance, and Income Protection, think long and hard about if you really need Critical Illness Coverage. Remember: insurance isn't a savings plan. If you already have these other covers, do you really need that lump sum in the event you're diagnosed with one of the specified illnesses or would that premium money be better used buying Assets?

A note of caution: please never, ever lie about your current health or conveniently forget to mention any specific medical condition or past condition on any of your insurance forms. This is particularly important when it comes to your Medical Insurance, Life Insurance, and Critical Illness application forms. Answer every single question honestly. Lying or omitting information about medical conditions is the single biggest reason that claims get rejected.

Imagine paying your premiums for years and years, only to discover you will not be receiving your claim because you chose not to mention the few cigarettes you sometimes have with a couple of drinks or because you didn't mention the one malignant melanoma you had removed years ago.

Don't presume something doesn't matter. Insurance companies love it when a person doesn't fully disclose. It doesn't matter if your claim has absolutely nothing to do with the matter you chose not to tell them about; they have the right to withhold your payout or reduce it significantly if they find out you withheld any information. So, pour your heart out and declare everything, even that ingrown toenail you had 15 years ago!

Once again, shop around for your Income and Critical Illness Insurance if you determine that you need these too.

Any other insurances?

If you have Life Insurance, Home Building Insurance, Contents Insurance, Medical Insurance (if required), Income, Disability, and Critical Illness Coverage, and Car Insurance, there are absolutely no other insurances you need—not domestic travel insurance, car rental insurance, loan insurance, appliance insurance, service contracts, mortgage life insurance, flight insurance, or funeral insurance. The list goes on. The insurance industry keeps coming up with yet another must-have policy for you to spend your wealth on.

These are all of marginal value at best and are usually a complete rip-off, designed to maximize the insurance industries' profits. The agents also tend to make huge commissions on these products, often as high as 60 percent, while you are typically overcharged by 200 to 800 percent for these horrible products!

Please, do not fall for the sales pitches and clever marketing, all just based on fear, which aim to separate you from your money for things you do not need.

Finally, make a Wealth Chef habit of reviewing all your insurance policies every year to ensure your coverage remains appropriate and adequate.

This was perhaps rather tough . . .

Well done! We've been through some topics we'd all rather not have to talk about but absolutely must take into consideration. Now you need to really have those conversations with yourself and those you love, and put together your Protection Pâté so you can rest assured that, no matter what, the people who depend on you will be well looked after financially.

Now, that is a great gift not just to them, but to you, too!

With all this safely stored in your Wealth Kitchen, now you can really focus your attention and energy on expanding your wealth!

Protection Pâté

LEVEL OF DIFFICULTY > Easy

. . . .

INGREDIENTS :

- Income Statement
- Balance Sheet

SKILLS REQUIRED :

- Internet searching
- Formfilling

TOOLS REQUIRED :

- Financial Freedom
  Feast Menu
- Rat Race Roast Amount

TIME REQUIRED :

- 3 hours initial setup
- 1 hour per year to review
  and amend

METHOD :

. . . .

Home Insurance >

1. Make an inventory of your household belongings.

2. Make an estimate of the current (new) replacement value.

3. Get three different quotes for Home Insurance coverage.

Vehicle Insurance >

1. Determine the type of Car Insurance you need: third-party only; third-party, fire & theft; or comprehensive.

2. Get a minimum of three quotes, including combined quotes for your home and other vehicles.

3. Choose a voluntary excess.

4. No fancy frills or add-ons.

Life Insurance >

1. Jot down the size of your Rat Race Roast Wealth Pot lump sum.

2. Subtract your current Net Worth from your Rat Race Roast lump sum amount.

Cont. >

3. The remaining lump sum represents the Life Insurance amount you require.

4. Determine the time period for which you need the Life Insurance to cover.

5. Get a minimum of three quotes for TERM life cover for the Life Insurance amount, and the time period for which you need it.

6. No fancy frills or add-ons.

7. Specify your beneficiaries.

Critical Illness and Disability Coverage >

1. Identify the Rat Race Roast Income required.

2. Get three quotes for Income Protection/Disability Coverage.

Review in a Year >

1. Review and update all your required insurance amounts.

2. Get new quotes for all your insurances.

3. Change Insurance provider if you get a better quote.

. . . .

Breathe out, sleep soundly, and focus on living richly and creating your Financial Freedom Feast, knowing you have a safety net for you and those who rely on you.

14

Wealth Recipe #5: Mastery

You've arrived at core Wealth Recipe #5. This is not only the final recipe you'll need in your financial freedom repertoire, but it's also the one I consider the most important. This is the recipe that holds all the others together and gives your whole Financial Freedom Feast its heart and soul.

Mastery is about becoming unconsciously competent at making, keeping, and growing money.

A few years ago, I wanted to learn how to play the guitar. I had visions of standing in front of an adoring crowd, who were cheering as my fingers flew up and down the strings, looking not dissimilar to Eric Clapton (on a bad, or a good day, I didn't mind). Oh, it was so exciting! I dashed out and bought the guitar, got my "Learn to Play in Five Easy Steps" CD and workbook, and settled down to master it.

It didn't take long for me to realize I was completely clueless at this guitar-playing business!

You see, I'd passed through the first stage of learning (Unconscious Incompetence) and very quickly hit the second stage of learning (Conscious Incompetence) with a big bang: I'd become all too conscious of my own incompetence. Sadly, this is where most people give up on their dreams: when they realize that they will take a bit of work.

According to best-selling Canadian author Malcolm Gladwell, mastery takes around 10,000 hours. But you can and will achieve significant success way before mastery, because your competence grows and increases with time. If you persist, if you put in the time and create a new set of habits, you'll quickly move to the third stage of learning, Conscious Competence.

This is when your wealth journey will seriously accelerate and things will become smoother, easier, and just plain old fun! And once you have this rolling, you'll effortlessly move onto the final stage of learning, mastery. This is the zone where you are Unconsciously Competent—that is, able to make, keep, and grow your money automatically, and effortlessly.

The journey to mastery

The journey to mastery requires massive action, commitment, new behaviors, a support team, and teachers. But it is worth every step because, after all, the journey leads you to *freedom*.

Learning guitar was not a "must" for me, and after the first wild burst of enthusiasm and the realization of my own incompetence, I stopped picking it up, and it now sits in the corner of my office, reminding me that enthusiasm alone isn't enough. Mastery requires action—and lots of it!

During the course of this book, you may have had thoughts along the lines of, "Oh, this is too hard," "I don't think I've got what it takes," "I'm not good at this kind of stuff," and so on. If this has happened, congratulations! You've already hit the Consciously Incompetent Level as regards your money skills. This is the critical point that separates the wannabes from the achievers. Most people give up on their dreams at precisely this point, but I know this isn't you because you've kept going right up to this point. If you were going to wimp out and give up on your dreams, you would have done it before now!

So now is the time to draw on all the internal resources I know you have, and recommit to mastering your money: to doing whatever it takes to stay on this journey and create the financial support you deserve in your life.

Whether I learned to play the guitar or not was never going to affect my being able to achieve the things I wanted to achieve in my life and experience the things I wanted to experience. And it certainly wasn't going to enable me to be, have, create, and achieve in the same way as having achieved financial freedom has done!

Creating my Financial Freedom Feast was a must, however. I wanted it! And I knew that not creating it, and not mastering the Wealth Recipes, would have destroyed my ability to live the life I wanted to live—the life I'm able to live now.

But just wanting it isn't enough either. I wanted it—I really did—but kept messing it up.

As you know, my father planted the seed of possibility, the desire to master my money, the need to take responsibility for my own wealth and ensure I could always look after myself financially. Unfortunately, he died before I had a chance to learn how to do it. Nevertheless, the seed within me grew and grew. After my initial escapade with store cards, bank loans, and debt, and my lucky escape from crippling consumer debt, I knew I had to save—I had to spend less than I earned to become rich. And so I saved, and I saved.

In my late twenties, I was living and working in Hong Kong and had technically saved enough money to be financially free. But there were two big problems: first, I didn't know the difference between saving and investing, and so the money had no way of doing what it's designed to do—grow—because I hadn't converted it into wealth-generating Assets; and second, I'd become completely obsessed with living on as little money as I could. I'd developed Money Anorexia.

As you now know, this wasn't wealth at all. I deprived my creative fun side more and more and prevented the money from expanding . . . a volcano was brewing. My world finally imploded when I turned thirty. I created a huge and messy drama in my life that cost me my marriage and all the money I'd saved. I didn't understand what had happened: one moment I was a married millionaire and the next, I had zero money and no husband. But something in me knew I hadn't yet discovered all the pieces; I hadn't yet found the key to sustainable wealth.

I knew I still needed to keep doing the "spend less than you earn" part—but now I had to find the missing recipes. I read books on investing and learned more and more about the scientific and technical aspects of improving the returns on my investments, and slowly my Net Worth began to grow again. But I knew I hadn't yet cracked the wealth code.

Then a cigarette changed my life.

What is a mentor?

I was standing smoking on a pavement outside my office in London and started eavesdropping on a conversation going on next to me: a woman and a man were having a very animated discussion about some training that they'd been on with some American chap I'd never heard of.

Quite frankly, it sounded a bit weird, but I couldn't stop listening because their energy was amazing—they just seemed so full of life! Without even thinking about it, I interrupted their conversation and asked them what they were they talking about with an excitement that was practically contagious. And they shared it with me.

That cigarette changed my life. You see, they were talking about an event with American author and business guru Tony Robbins. I immediately walked across the street and bought his book. In it, I discovered the most incredible concept: the idea that if something isn't working in our lives, we can change it, not by changing it from the outside but by going inside ourselves and changing that first—by using skills to reprogram who we are. Robbins was saying that we can define our own destiny by mastering the greatest power on earth: our own minds.

Well, that just blew me away! So I decided to use the skills I was learning from the book to stop smoking first, and then my husband Dave and I started the most amazing journey of all: the journey of self-mastery. I believe this is the most rewarding and fulfilling journey anyone can choose to embark on.

It's a journey of a lifetime and it does take a lifetime! It isn't always easy, and it's often not pretty, but it is always amazing. I realized learning should not end after you finish university, but rather it should be a lifelong pursuit. And I discovered that the biggest investment I needed to make was in me—for this is where I would find the secret to my financial freedom.

Tony Robbins was my first mentor. Since those heady days of my first live seminar with him, I've had numerous other mentors and teachers. I continue to do so, and I believe I always will. I bring teachers into my life in each area where I want to grow and learn. I attend seminars regularly and continue to expand the best wealth-creating vehicle ever: myself!

I can't explain the money mechanics of it all. But I do know that once I started mastering myself, my wealth went stratospheric. I uncovered my disempowering money beliefs—some pretty messed-up and conflicting values about having money in my life—and learned the skills to retune them so as to support, rather than sabotage, my goals. I also learned the power of my mind to create my own reality and realized that I could have the life of my dreams—not sometime in the future, but now.

In the year after getting my first mentor, Tony Robbins, my salary doubled—and in the same job where I'd been, before I'd started investing in me! I simply became better and more effective in all areas of my life.

In the next two years, my Income quadrupled, despite the fact that I took six months off with Dave to train with some amazing mentors, attend property investing, equity investing, and personal growth seminars, and also just have some fun. We also moved countries and jobs in that time, and besides the exponential growth in my Income, I was offered positions that enabled me to grow significantly personally and help others!

As my Income grew, I got better and better at managing, keeping, and growing my money. My investment returns increased every year. My Wealth Pots grew faster and faster. As a result, I became financially free: I achieved Course 6 (Financial Freedom Flambé, on the Financial Freedom Menu) in just six years after I started my personal mastery journey and only eight after starting over again in Hong Kong!

But it wasn't until I discovered I had to go inside first, and invest in myself, that I finally understood the difference between being rich and being wealthy.

Money grows when it's given the right environment— it's just what it does—in the same way as night follows day and Orion chases Scorpio across the night sky. But the Chef is the one who turns money into wealth. The Chef gives meaning to money and creates the feast. The Chef is the person who makes the difference—and that Chef is you! How abundant your feast is depends on the type of Chef you become.

So, please, commit to mastering *you*!

You do this by following the fifth and final Recipe for Wealth—Mastery.

A four-piece puzzle

Mastery is a four-piece puzzle, and when you learn how to put the pieces together, you'll have cracked the code to real, sustainable wealth. If you apply this final recipe in your life, it will accelerate your financial freedom journey exponentially. This is the recipe that will give you the skills you need to stay on the most fantastic journey you'll ever take: the journey to financial freedom and true personal wealth.

- Piece 1 -
Your obsession

Create and maintain a compelling, juicy, tantalizing future that pulls you toward your Big Why and your Financial Freedom Feast Vision. (And if you haven't created them yet, do so now!)

Maybe you feel it's all a bit woo-woo and you'll just stick with the technical aspects of this money business? Well, I've been there and done that, and yes, you may achieve financial success without it, but not at the speed and with the sustainability that you will with this critical piece. So, keep your vision alive by stepping into it each and every morning. See it in your life now. Feel your vision in every cell of your body, hear the sounds in it, and keep turning it up, making it juicier, richer, more yummy every day, until it becomes your obsession.

- Piece 2 -
The master system

Commit to mastering your mind. Discover your internal workings and check if your current operating system is supporting or sabotaging your dreams.

The average person spends an incredible amount of time with his or her brain switched off, often staring at one of the biggest wealth vampires there is: the TV. Please switch the box off and switch on your neck-top computer instead!

Learn how to create a set of sieves (beliefs, values, rules, and identity) that will help you thrive. And master your molders of meaning (your language, focus, and physiology) so that the effect of your actions is none other than the life you deserve.

You've already had a taste of how powerful your sieves are and you're already mastering your molders of meaning, by the quality questions you ask yourself now.

Uncover your current wealth values and see if you have any conflicting ones, as most of us do (I certainly did!), and then learn how to realign them to support your Financial Freedom Vision.

- Piece 3 -
The influencers

Tony Robbins says we become whom we spend most of our time with. So, be exceptionally discerning about who and what you choose to spend your most precious resource—time—on. Make sure the external influences in your life add to your Wealth Feast, instead of hampering it! Fill your life with mentors, teachers, information, and friends who support your vision.

Take my case: I've always enjoyed being active, but I confess I find it difficult to get myself to actually exercise! I know I must do it, I know I feel good when I do so, and I also know that it plays a key role in my overall well-being. But I haven't yet managed to make exercise and health an automatic part of the things I just "do." So, recognizing that I don't yet have this sorted in the same way as I have my money management and wealth creation habits, I get help. I don't beat myself up about it; I simply acknowledge that I'm on a mastery journey in relation to fitness and that, while on the journey, I need a master to help me get there!

So I have a personal trainer who works with me to ensure I do the things I need to do in order to stay fit and healthy. I also know that, with time, I'll get to the point where the habit of exercising will become a part of who I am, and I may not need him anymore.

I also know that once I achieve my current fitness goals, I may then choose to take my health and fitness to a new level that I hadn't previously imagined, and so I may continue with this teacher, or find a new one who can take me there.

In addition to your mentors, your peer group is crucial. Did you know that your Income will be within 10 to 15 percent of the Income of the three or four people you spend the most time with? We all have an enormous need to belong, and so we will unconsciously do whatever it takes to fit in with the people we spend the most time with—even if that means not allowing money to stay in our lives!

So choose your friends wisely and ensure you always have a few people in your life who are doing better than you are, in whatever area. This is important! That way, you'll keep expanding in order to fit in—rather than playing small.

- Piece 4 -
The key of knowledge

Keep expanding your knowledge in all areas of wealth. Master each of the four Asset groups: Property Investing, Equity Investing, Passive Income Businesses, and You.

I recommend you keep investing in your index trackers and select one specialty area to expand your knowledge in first. Grow your skills in this specific area, learn what you need to learn, apply it, and grow that part of your wealth. And then move on to the next specialty area.

Your goal is to have investments in all four Asset groups, so that not only is your Asset Drawer filling up faster, but you also have your risks spread between different investment sectors.

As your investment skills and wealth knowledge grow, so will the rate of return that you're able to create. The rate at which you're able to grow your money is in direct proportion to your competence. Remember the exponential impact just a few percentage points' difference in the rate of return has on the speed with which you achieve financial freedom, or the speed with which bad debt can drag you down to money hell?

The simple objective of a Wealth Chef is to create a Financial Freedom Feast—and to do that, you must convert active Income into wealth-generating Assets. How much you convert, how quickly you convert it, how well you convert it, and how effectively you're able to make the Assets work will determine how quickly you'll reach your objective.

The Key of Knowledge not only increases the rate at which you'll achieve your feast, but it also fuels your mastery itself—because nothing fuels mastery like success. So every time you learn something new and apply it, celebrate! Acknowledge how far you've come and how much you've learned. And soon that effort and skill will be reflected in your Balance Sheet.

There you have it!

These are the four pieces of Wealth Recipe #5—Mastery. Unlike the previous recipes, mastery is not a step-by-step linear process, but rather a never-ending wonderful journey of expansion. It needs each of the four pieces to grow and expand, so that the whole stays together. The more you work on expanding and mastering you, the quicker you'll achieve your Financial Freedom Feast. I truly believe this is one of the greatest investments you can make—without it, you may bring money into your life but not wealth.

Mastery

LEVEL OF DIFFICULTY > Moderate

. . . .

INGREDIENTS:

- *You*
- *Your peer group*
- *Your mentors*

TOOLS REQUIRED:

- *Your Big Why*
- *Your Financial Freedom Vision*

SKILLS REQUIRED:

- *Perseverance*
- *Belief, commitment*

TIME REQUIRED:

- *A lifetime of discovery*

METHOD:

. . . .

The Obsession > Create and maintain a compelling future that pulls you toward it with your Big Why and your juicy Financial Freedom Feast Vision.

The Master System > Commit to mastering you. Discover your internal workings and how your current system is either supporting or sabotaging your dreams.

Learn how to create a set of sieves (beliefs, values, rules, and identity) that help you thrive and master your molders of meaning so that your decisions and actions create the life you deserve.

The Influencers > Ensure the external influences in your life add to your wealth and don't diminish it. Fill your life with mentors, teachers, friends, food, and information that support your vision.

Growth > Keep expanding your knowledge in all areas of wealth: Property Investing, Equity Investing, Passive Income Businesses, as well as your Active Income.

. . . .

Flourish as your wealth unfolds easily and effortlessly, now that you've discovered the code!

15.

A Marathon or a Sprint?

Congratulations! You've mastered the recipes, you know just what it is that you're creating, and you also know how large your Wealth Pots need to be. But how long is this going to take? How long is it going to take you to create your Financial Freedom Feast and finally become financially free?

You're now about to discover not only how long it will take you to achieve each course in your Wealth Feast, but you're also going to have a great tool, which will show you the impact of investing more money each month, as well as the impact of using the Wealth Accelerators, time, and interest rate.

You'll need the following:

- Your Financial Freedom Feast Menu with your target Net Worth Wealth Pots for each course

- The amount you're putting into your Investment Pot

- Your current Balance Sheet, which tells you where you are right now (i.e., your current Net Worth)

- Your Financial Freedom Feast Cooking Timer Spreadsheet from the Wealth Chef website (see the link at the end of the book):

In the columns, there are different rates of return (interest rates) and, down the side, blank spaces for you to fill in. Only fill in the highlighted blocks and then see the impact of different monthly investment amounts and interest rates, to see how long it will take to achieve your vision.

Start with the first highlighted block, the Base Amount, and fill in your current Net Worth. In the second block, put the regular monthly investment amount that you've committed to. This is the amount that you're putting into your Investment Pot each month. In this example we start with an amount of $100,000 and add a "pay yourself first" amount of $1,000 a month.

Then, from your Financial Freedom Feast Menu, add the target Net Worth amount that you need to create your Security Soup, your Vital Veggies, your Rat Race Roast, and finally your Financial Freedom Flambé. This will tell you what you're aiming for in terms of Net Worth for each of the courses.

Next, start going down the column under the 8 percent interest rate, until you find the value closest to your Rat Race Roast target—the amount of money needed to complete your Rat Race Roast.

When you arrive at it, you'll see in the column under the header "YEARS," how many years your current regular investment amount and your current Net Worth will take to achieve that amount of money, assuming you achieve an average 8 percent rate of return.

In the example, a Rat Race Roast Net Worth target of, say, 1.5 million would take 24 years to achieve with an 8 percent rate of return and a monthly contribution of $1,000.

As you go across the columns to the right, you'll see that the number of years to achieve the same amount with 10 percent interest is a lot less, and with 12 percent interest, even less so, and so on and so forth. As your rate of return increases, so the amount of time it takes to achieve that target lessens significantly.

Also play around with your regular investment amount: increase the amount and see the difference it makes in the time needed to achieve your Wealth Feast goals and targets. The more you put into your wealth pot and the higher your investment rate of return is, the faster you'll achieve financial freedom.

This tells you exactly how quickly you're going to achieve your targets with different rates of returns and investment amounts. That is, how many years it will take you to achieve each Wealth Feast target at different "pay yourself first" amounts and interest rates.

As I set my wealth targets, I realized I didn't want to wait 24 years to be financially free. So I needed to increase both my monthly contribution into my Wealth Pots and the rate of return I was getting. I needed to make my money work harder.

- TIME-TO-FREEDOM TRACKER I -		Rate of Return Interest Rate	
FILL IN THE SHADED BLOCKS ONLY >	Years	8%	10%
	1	$120,960	$123,200
	2	143,597	148,720
	3	168,045	176,792
Base (Start) Amount	$100,000	4	194,448	207,671
Regular Investment (Monthly)	1,000	5	222,964	241,638
Regular investment (Annually)	12,000	6	253,761	279,002
	7	287,022	320,102
	8	322,944	365,313
Security Soup Target	9	361,739	415,044
Vital Veggie Target	10	403,638	469,748
Rat Race Roast Target	11	448,889	529,923
Freedom Flambé Target	12	497,761	596,115
	13	550,541	668,927
Years to Security Soup	14	607,545	749,020
Years to Vital Veggies	15	669,108	837,122
Years to Rat Race Roast	16	735,597	934,034
Years to Freedom Flambé	17	807,405	1,040,637
	18	884,957	1,157,901
	19	968,714	1,286,891
	20	1,059,171	1,428,780
	21	1,156,864	1,584,858
	22	1,262,374	1,756,544
	23	1,376,323	1,945,398
	24	1,499,389	2,153,138
	25	1,632,301	2,381,652
	26	1,775,845	2,633,017
	27	1,930,872	2,909,519
	28	2,098,302	3,213,671
	29	2,279,126	3,548,238
	30	2,474,416	3,916,261
	31	2,685,329	4,321,087
	32	2,913,116	4,766,396
	33	3,159,125	5,256,236
	34	3,424,815	5,795,059
	35	3,711,760	6,387,765
	36	4,021,661	7,039,742
	37	4,356,354	7,756,916
	38	4,717,822	8,545,808
	39	5,108,208	9,413,588
	40	5,529,825	10,368,147

	Rate of Return Interest Rate			
Years	12%	15%	20%	25%
1	$125,440	$128,800	$134,400	$140,000
2	153,933	161,920	175,680	190,000
3	185,845	200,008	225,216	252,500
4	221,586	243,809	284,659	330,625
5	261,616	294,181	355,991	428,281
6	306,450	352,108	441,589	550,352
7	356,664	418,724	544,307	702,939
8	412,904	495,332	667,569	893,674
9	475,893	583,432	815,482	1,132,093
10	546,440	684,747	992,979	1,430,116
11	625,453	801,259	1,205,974	1,802,645
12	713,947	935,248	1,461,569	2,268,306
13	813,061	1,089,335	1,768,283	2,850,383
14	924,068	1,266,536	2,136,340	3,577,979
15	1,048,396	1,470,316	2,578,008	4,487,474
16	1,187,643	1,704,663	3,108,009	5,624,342
17	1,343,601	1,974,163	3,744,011	7,045,427
18	1,518,273	2,284,087	4,507,213	8,821,784
19	1,713,905	2,640,500	5,423,056	11,042,230
20	1,933,014	3,050,375	6,522,067	13,817,788
21	2,178,416	3,521,731	7,840,881	17,287,235
22	2,453,266	4,063,791	9,423,457	21,624,043
23	2,761,098	4,687,160	11,322,548	27,045,054
24	3,105,869	5,404,034	13,601,458	33,821,318
25	3,492,014	6,228,439	16,336,149	42,291,647
26	3,924,495	7,176,505	19,617,779	52,879,559
27	4,408,875	8,266,780	23,555,735	66,114,449
28	4,951,380	9,520,598	28,281,282	82,658,061
29	5,558,985	10,962,487	33,951,938	103,337,577
30	6,239,503	12,620,660	40,756,726	129,186,971
31	7,001,684	14,527,559	48,922,471	161,498,713
32	7,855,326	16,720,493	58,721,365	201,888,392
33	8,811,405	19,242,367	70,480,038	252,375,490
34	9,882,214	22,142,522	84,590,446	315,484,362
35	11,081,519	25,477,700	101,522,935	394,370,453
36	12,424,742	29,313,156	121,841,922	492,978,066
37	13,929,151	33,723,929	146,224,707	616,237,582
38	15,614,089	38,796,318	175,484,048	770,311,978
39	17,501,219	44,629,566	210,595,258	962,904,972
40	19,614,806	51,337,801	252,728,710	1,203,646,215

- TIME-TO-FREEDOM TRACKER 2 -		Years	Rate of Return Interest Rate	
FILL IN THE HIGHLIGHTED BLOCKS ONLY >			8%	10%
		1	$140,400	$143,000
		2	184,032	190,300
		3	231,155	242,330
Base (Start) Amount	$100,000	4	282,047	299,563
Regular Investment (Monthly)	2,500	5	337,011	362,519
Regular investment (Annually)	30,000	6	396,372	431,771
		7	460,481	507,948
		8	529,720	591,743
Security Soup Target		9	604,497	683,918
Vital Veggie Target		10	685,257	785,309
Rat Race Roast Target		11	772,478	896,840
Freedom Flambé Target		12	866,676	1,019,524
		13	968,410	1,154,477
Years to Security Soup		14	1,078,283	1,302,924
Years to Vital Veggies		15	1,196,945	1,466,217
Years to Rat Race Roast		16	1,325,101	1,645,838
Years to Freedom Flambé		17	1,463,509	1,843,422
		18	1,612,990	2,060,764
		19	1,774,429	2,299,841
		20	1,948,783	2,562,825
		21	2,137,086	2,852,107
		22	2,340,453	3,170,318
		23	2,560,089	3,520,350
		24	2,797,296	3,905,385
		25	3,053,480	4,328,924
		26	3,330,158	4,794,816
		27	3,628,971	5,307,298
		28	3,951,689	5,871,027
		29	4,300,224	6,491,130
		30	4,676,642	7,173,243
		31	5,083,173	7,923,567
		32	5,522,227	8,748,924
		33	5,996,405	9,656,816
		34	6,508,517	10,655,498
		35	7,061,599	11,754,048
		36	7,658,927	12,962,453
		37	8,304,041	14,291,698
		38	9,000,764	15,753,868
		39	9,753,225	17,362,254
		40	10,565,883	19,131,480

	Rate of Return Interest Rate			
Years	12%	15%	20%	25%
1	$145,600	$149,500	$156,000	$162,500
2	196,672	206,425	223,200	240,625
3	253,873	271,889	303,840	338,281
4	317,937	347,172	400,608	460,352
5	389,690	433,748	516,730	612,939
6	470,053	533,310	656,076	803,674
7	560,059	647,807	823,291	1,042,093
8	660,866	779,478	1,023,949	1,340,116
9	773,770	930,899	1,264,738	1,712,645
10	900,222	1,105,034	1,553,686	2,178,306
11	1,041,849	1,305,289	1,900,423	2,760,383
12	1,200,471	1,535,583	2,316,508	3,487,979
13	1,378,127	1,800,420	2,815,810	4,397,474
14	1,577,103	2,104,983	3,414,972	5,534,342
15	1,799,955	2,455,230	4,133,966	6,955,427
16	2,049,550	2,858,015	4,996,759	8,731,784
17	2,329,096	3,321,217	6,032,111	10,952,230
18	2,642,187	3,853,900	7,274,533	13,727,788
19	2,992,849	4,466,485	8,765,440	17,197,235
20	3,385,591	5,170,957	10,554,528	21,534,043
21	3,825,462	5,981,101	12,701,434	26,955,054
22	4,318,118	6,912,766	15,277,720	33,731,318
23	4,869,892	7,984,181	18,369,264	42,201,647
24	5,487,879	9,216,308	22,079,117	52,789,559
25	6,180,024	10,633,254	26,530,941	66,024,449
26	6,955,227	12,262,743	31,873,129	82,568,061
27	7,823,455	14,136,654	38,283,755	103,247,577
28	8,795,869	16,291,652	45,976,505	129,096,971
29	9,884,974	18,769,900	55,207,807	161,408,713
30	11,104,770	21,619,885	66,285,368	201,798,392
31	12,470,943	24,897,367	79,578,441	252,285,490
32	14,001,056	28,666,473	95,530,130	315,394,362
33	15,714,783	33,000,943	114,672,156	394,280,453
34	17,634,157	37,985,585	137,642,587	492,888,066
35	19,783,855	43,717,923	165,207,104	616,147,582
36	22,191,518	50,310,111	198,284,525	770,221,978
37	24,888,100	57,891,128	237,977,430	962,814,972
38	27,908,272	66,609,297	285,608,916	1,203,556,215
39	31,290,865	76,635,192	342,766,699	1,504,482,769
40	35,079,369	88,164,970	411,356,039	1,880,640,961

Looking at our combined Income Statement, Dave and I decided to live on one Income and invest the whole of my Income in our future. This amounted to an after-tax amount of around $2,500 a month. Even at an 8 percent rate of return, this made a huge difference to my "time to freedom," bringing it down to just 17 years.

But I am impatient! To make it quicker, I needed to increase the rate of return. By mastering the different Asset groups and becoming better and better at investing, I now average a rate of return of around 20 percent on my investments. As you can see, that reduces the time to freedom to under ten years.

If you follow everything you've read in this book, and keep investing in your index tracker, you should achieve an average rate of return across the whole portfolio of around 11 percent per annum—because over time this is what markets have returned since records have been kept. The time it takes to achieve your Wealth Feast at this rate of return may be absolutely fine for you—or not. Remember, though, that this is a marathon, not a sprint, and simply knowing that you're going to achieve it is totally awesome!

If you want to achieve financial freedom sooner, you'll need to put more money into your wealth pot each and every month and also achieve higher rates of return. You can see from the example the difference adding additional money into your Wealth Pots and what a higher rate of return make to your Wealth Feast and to the time it takes for you to achieve your financial freedom goal.

You achieve higher rates of return by increasing your financial and wealth literacy and knowledge; by applying the Wealth Cooking accelerators of compounding and leverage; and by mastering the gourmet Wealth Cooking specialities—property investing, more sophisticated stock market investing, developing passive and residual Income businesses, and expanding you.

Isn't investing risky?

I'm often asked about risk—about investing being risky. After the housing crash and the stock market crash in 2008, there are more people than ever who will tell you that investing is risky.

The problem is that not everyone defines "investing" in the same way.

Most people think of investing as any situation where you put down money with the expectation of getting a return on it. Unfortunately, what many people think of as investing is actually gambling! This is why so many people have been burned by those events.

Many so-called investors bought into the real estate market when it was hot and prices were soaring, and they invested in the hope that home values would keep going up and up, even taking on properties that cost more to buy and maintain than they could be rented for.

On the other hand, experienced investors who understood the fundamentals of real estate investing refused to buy houses that didn't have a positive cash flow (i.e., that would not generate Income to cover the properties' costs, including the interest on the mortgages), and sold properties they'd bought before the boom for a nice profit.

In any kind of investing, what sets a gambler apart from the true Wealth Chef is the understanding of the fundamentals, and having a solid level-four Wealth Chef foundation in place. Knowing and following the fundamentals takes much of the risk out of investing. There is always some, but by sticking to sound investment strategies and planning for ways to cover the downside, the risks can be greatly reduced.

So make your foundations solid, learn the fundamentals, start small, gain experience, and you, too can become a Gourmet Wealth Chef!

This is what the final chapter is all about— Momentum—and it's about staying the course on the road less traveled. You'll discover how to make your new wealth habits a part of your life, so you don't lose all the amazing progress you've made, and you'll learn how to do so in such a way that, with time, it simply becomes a part of who you are.

16.

Momentum

So much has happened in the last 15 chapters! I really want to honor you for keeping up, for putting in not only the time but also the emotional commitment, and for deciding to make wealth—your wealth—a priority in your life.

Thank you also for your trust. We've been together on this journey for a while now: you've been doing the wealth focus exercises, creating your Wealth Kitchen tools, managing your money, and mastering the recipes.

You've been creating new wealthy habits. Whether you're aware of them consciously or unconsciously, they're now a part of you! This is a very important start, a huge step on your financial freedom journey.

You now have all the tools you need.

But, and it's a big *but*, you must keep making your wealth a priority in your life, keeping up the momentum you've created, and continuing to grow not only your wealth but also yourself.

You must continue on your wealth mastery journey, growing and refining your skills, your ability to bring more money into your life, to manage significantly larger amounts of money and have more of it stay with you, and to achieve higher investment returns.

Wealth is like health. It's something you need to keep creating and choosing, over and over again. So many people try to find the one-hit wonder, the big payday, the lottery win, the magic system, believing that then they'll finally be rich. This is like thinking you can go to the gym just once, pop a few omega oil tablets, and you'll be fit and healthy and have all the energy you need forever—even if you go back to binging on mountains of sugar and Super-Size-Me Mac meals and never get off the couch!

So this is what this final chapter is all about: momentum. How to keep your new wealth habits, so you don't lose all the amazing progress you've made. And how to do so in such a way that, with time, they simply become a part of your life.

The first key to momentum is within you—it's all about your identity and who you believe you are.

Identity

Identity is one of our strongest drivers: we are what we think our identity is. We'll do almost anything to remain consistent with our own identities—the things that we believe about ourselves. If your identify is one of wealth; financial mastery; being great with making, keeping, and growing money, your actions will reflect that and your results will reinforce who you think you are—in other words, your identity.

Identity is one of the key components of the internal sieves we all have, which we talked about in Chapter 6. Remember this phrase: "You will see it when you believe it." Most people say "I'll believe it, when I see it." This is backwards thinking, and until you fully understand that the believing comes first, wealth will elude you.

What you believe about yourself is the most important of all your beliefs and when you believe "I'm great with money," "Money stays in my life," "Having money in my life is good," "Growing and investing money is easy," and so on, you'll see your wealth expanding rapidly.

Notice the things you say about yourself, to yourself, and to others. When you notice a self-identifier that doesn't serve you or your wealth, quickly jot it down and find a character trait completely opposite to it, aligned to who you need to be in order to achieve financial freedom. Then create a phrase to say to yourself (for example, about your becoming more and more like the desired identity every day), and repeat it, over and over again. Write it down too. At first this will seem totally weird, but with time you'll start finding evidence to support your new wealthy identity.

For example, one of my clients consistently told me, "Oh, Ann—I'm useless with numbers—I can't even add!" Now, this belief about herself was seriously impairing her ability to create wealth. And because she needed to stay consistent with her identity ("I'm useless with numbers!"), she never got past Go whenever she tried to create her Wealth Tools.

We worked on this. First, by making her aware of her language, so that she could catch herself whenever she was on the verge of repeating this belief, and then quickly overriding it by saying to herself instead, "I'm getting better and better with numbers every day."

Notice the language she used. If she'd suddenly tried to tell herself, "I'm just like Einstein—brilliant with numbers!" her mind would have laughed itself silly. But because the phrase was one of movement toward her desired identity, it was totally believable—and so her mind cooperated to make it so.

So, identify the character traits—the identity—of the person you need to become. Come up with four or five strong, clear virtues and work on making them a part of you.

For example: focused, great at numbers, determined, joyful, and grateful.

Then work on ways to make these a part of who you are.

TIPS

- A great technique for doing this is by creating an affirmation for yourself, something like:

- "Every day I'm becoming more focused; great at numbers; even more determined, joyful, and grateful; and my wealth expands in my life easily and effortlessly."

- Say this to yourself over and over again; say it to yourself while you travel to work, while you exercise, while you shower—whenever and wherever you can. Write it out in your journal every day and notice how it becomes more and more true.

The five laws of wealth

The second key of momentum is understanding and applying the Five Laws of Wealth. You must learn how to have them work in your life so that creating, keeping, and growing your wealth becomes significantly easier.

Understanding and applying these laws of wealth is the difference between power and force. It's what differentiates your financial freedom journey between being an uphill struggle or a grand, exciting adventure. And if you haven't yet read the book of the same name—*Power vs. Force*, by David Hawkins—do yourself a favor and read it!

- Wealth Law 1 -
The law of cause and effect

You learned all about this law when you mastered Protection Pâté. This is about choosing to live your life at "cause," about taking responsibility for everything in your life, good or bad, and, as a result, having the option to do something about it.

- Wealth Law 2 -
The law of emanation
(also known as: Perception Is Projection)

Picture this: you're at a traffic light and a red Ferrari pulls up next to you. Sitting in the driver's seat is a man in his mid-50s, his hair thinning on top. He's got a bit of a belly, and a stunning, sexy woman seated next to him. She's beautifully coiffed and manicured and is wearing an outfit to die for, topped off with stunning sunglasses and gorgeous jewelry.

Notice what thoughts come into your head. What do you think about the man, about the woman? What's their story?

Whatever you and I think about ourselves, deep down inside, is what we project onto the outside world. Whatever comment we make about others is also a comment about ourselves, as we can't perceive something in others that we don't ourselves have. So if you're noticing things in other people you don't like, you must first understand that the scratch is on the lens of your camera!

So the next time you see someone who is successful and wealthy, celebrate it! The next time you see someone who seems to be struggling with a challenge, don't feel sorry for him but, rather, see him for the excellent being he is, in control of his destiny, with all the resources he needs to achieve whatever he wants.

- Wealth Law 3 -
The law of meaning

We touched on the Law of Meaning when you learned about your molders of meaning—that the meaning we give something determines the decisions we make.

There are always choices in life, and life changes the minute you decide to make a different choice. Decision is the ultimate power. We've all been at big crossroads where we had to make a critical choice and we often think that these are the decisions that shape our lives. The truth is that we make three decisions every minute, and it's these decisions that shape our destiny, so the better we become at making decisions, the faster we reach our desired destiny.

A different decision means a different life. If you want a quality life, you need to make quality decisions.

What's the quality decision you need to make to keep your financial freedom growing?

- Wealth Law 4 -
The law of vacuums

What does a black hole do? It sucks everything into it. Imagine you could create a black hole in your life and point it toward all the goals you wanted to fill it up with. Wouldn't that be great?

In life, a vacuum is created whenever there is a "must." Here's an example: there are loads of things you say you want, but you either never get around to doing or buying them, or you tell yourself you don't have the money. But what if your car breaks down? If this is your only means of getting around and earning an Income, you now have a "must" and, somehow, you find the money. In just the same way, you need to make your financial freedom a "must."

You create a vacuum in two ways: first, by taking a giant leap of faith and leaving a void in your wake that literally pulls all your dreams into it; and second, by clearing out clutter in your life that's blocking new dreams and preventing goals from emerging. I recommend you keep doing both.

To take a giant leap requires movement. If there's no movement, there's no void. American business philosopher Jim Rhone said, "Successful people are willing to do what unsuccessful people are not willing to do." After all, you can set yourself a goal and then do nothing—then it remains just a dream. What are you willing to do that other people aren't? What giant leap of faith are you going to make to create the void needed to bring financial freedom into your life?

Just the other day, I was chatting with my twin brother and he reminded me about when we decided to work on our first property development together. Although we'd run all the numbers and knew it was a fantastic investment, neither of us had a clue as to how we were going to pay for it. But we took a giant leap. We committed to the project and created a vacuum— that is, we took massive action and we pulled in all the resources we needed. To date, it remains one of my best investments ever!

Clearing out clutter in all areas of your life is also vital: if you're holding on to things, physically, emotionally, or mentally, you need to clear them out. Make room in your life for the things you want.

Tackle just one room in your home, perhaps just one cupboard. Notice if you experience some resistance to throwing things out. The need to hoard and hold on to things you don't use (and hence don't get value from) is a clear sign of some scarcity beliefs that are affecting your ability to create and keep wealth in your life. Holding on to stuff that isn't serving you and from which you get little or no value is also a most effective braking system: it will grind your journey to financial freedom to a shuddering halt.

By taking giant leaps of faith and constantly clearing out the things that don't serve you any longer, you'll be able to speed things up!

- Wealth Law 5 -
The law of energy

There's a difference between energy and effort. To put in energy without expending effort makes all the difference between a full life and a busy life.

When most people try to succeed in their goals, what do they do? They work harder. If effort had anything to do with success, then successful people would be exhausted all the time and poor people would be bouncing off the walls with joyous energy. It's the other way around.

This is a difficult concept to describe. Like carrying a cup of coffee across a room, if you focus too hard and pay too much attention to the coffee, you'll spill it, but if you don't pay it any attention at all, you'll also spill it! There is a zone in between: enough but not too much.

So here's the paradox: the more effort you put into something, the more energy you're going to lose; and the more energy you put into something, the more effortless it becomes.

I'm sure you've had a day when you had loads of things to do and got it all done. How did you feel at the end of that day? Awesome! As the saying goes: if you want something done, give it to a busy person.

I'm equally sure you've also had a day where you didn't have much to do and didn't get any of it done. At the end of a day like this, how did you feel? Totally exhausted.

This has everything to do with the Law of Energy: incompletions drain energy, completions restore energy.

Incompletions drain energy from your psyche. Let me give you an example: a house falling apart. Let's imagine a clean, tidy home (we'll call it a "complete home") and, in a matter of days, your complete home gets turned upside down: it looks as if a tornado had hit it and you feel exhausted just looking at it. How did it happen? It usually starts in the kitchen ("I'll just leave the dishes for tomorrow"). Next morning, you get some breakfast (the last bowl in the cupboard, damn it!) and you run out of the house.

Being away lets you forget about it all day, but when you arrive back home, walk into the kitchen, and see the sink, wham! The sight hits you and down goes your energy. Now you are just too tired to cook, and anyway there are no clean plates, let alone pots and pans. So you reach for the phone ("Hello, Happy Pizza Deliveries!"), and sprawl across the sofa, feeling exhausted. You now have one empty pizza box and several paper napkins staring at you. Do you throw them away? No—you can't be bothered. Yes, I've been to your house—I did my research!

Completions restore energy to your psyche.

Let's look at your house again. Have you ever experienced this: despite feeling totally exhausted, the mess has just gotten to be too much, so you decide to clean up? You start in the bathroom (usually, it being the smallest room in the house has something to do with this!). How do you feel once you've got that one little room clean? "I think I'll just do a little more." And so you decide to tackle another room. At each completion, boom! Energy is restored! Soon enough, you're whizzing around an immaculately tidy and clean home like a maniac looking for things to do.

We need to get complete with whatever is incomplete in our lives in order to restore energy. Incompletions are not just physical things; they're also emotional. And debt is a huge incompletion.

There are three ways to complete things:

1. **Just do it**. Stop procrastinating and complete it!

2. **Schedule a time to complete it and then follow through with that time and actually do it when you said you would.** This is not procrastination. Look at debt. If you just say you'll pay off your debt when you can, then that is an incompletion. However, if you put your Debt Destroyer Plan in place, schedule it, and stick to it, you'll have just done a massive completion. Even if it takes you five years, if you stick to your plan, you'll get energy from destroying your debt, rather than feeling drained by it.

3. **Declare it complete and throw it away.** Just say to yourself, "I deem it complete." That phone call you've been meaning to make for years—deem it done; that article you meant to read—throw it away, let it go; those old bank accounts that you've kept open, just in case—close them; that relationship that ended but you've still held on to in some way—declare it over.

A great way to do this is to write all those things on a piece of paper and have a completion ceremony where you burn them all and let them go. (However, you can't do this with debt!)

Go through your home, your work space, and your mind and make a list of all your current incompletions. Keep adding to your list as things pop up. Looking at your list, find something you can just deem complete, cross it off, and notice the rise in your energy.

Once a week, go over this list, and mark a 1, 2, or 3 next to each item: for all the 1's—just do it; for all the 2's—schedule a time to do it; and for all the 3's—let them go!

Make it a habit

As you know, it's the things we do over and over again that determine where we end up, and a great deal of the work you've done while completing this book has been about creating wealth habits.

You also need to create time in your life to do the money things you need to do, such as updating your Wealth Tools (your Income Statement and Balance Sheet), reviewing your insurances, and researching new investments.

To that end, I've created a Wealth Cooking Calendar for you, detailing the monthly, quarterly, six-monthly, and annual activities you need to schedule in your life, in order to keep your wealth flowing. You can download a copy from The Wealth Chef website or make a copy of the one at the end of this book.

You'll also find a checklist of all the tasks you've been entrusted with throughout the book: your Wealth Kitchen Inventory. This gives you a quick and easy reference to check what you already have in place and what areas still need some work.

Keep going!

You've already begun creating your Financial Freedom Feast, so the hardest work has already been done: you've dug down deep and your foundations are now taking shape and form. Keep going! Continue to apply and master the five core Wealth Recipes, stick with what you've begun, and keep building on it.

Continue to seek knowledge and explore the vast array of opportunities to create wealth, knowing that wealth is available to everyone, that everyone is worthy of financial freedom, and that all you have to do is be open to it and take action!

If I've achieved only one thing in this book, I hope I've given you a spark, a taste of that awesome power of the Universe inside you, and a knowledge that financial freedom is meant for you! A taste of the truth that:

- Money will be with you wherever you go
- Success will be with you all the time
- Wealth will flow faster and faster
- You have to take those leaps, and . . .
- You have to let your light shine!

At one of my Wealth Weekender events, a woman came up to me in tears. She said, "Ann, I just don't see how I can feel good about having a lot of money when others have so little." I empathized with her, because I had also been crippled by the same very dis-empowering belief. Because I'd been there myself, I was able to help. I asked her a few simple questions: "What good do you do for poor people by being one of them? Whom do you help by being broke? Aren't you then just another mouth to feed, another person someone else must look after? Wouldn't it be more effective for you to create wealth for yourself and then be able to really help others from a place of strength instead of weakness?"

If you have the wherewithal to have a great deal of money, then have it! Why? Because the truth is that we are extremely fortunate to be living in a society whereby each person has the freedom to be whatever they desire, a freedom that was hard-fought for by many amazing people.

Love,
Ann

Appendix 1
The Wealth Chef Kitchen

KITCHEN INVENTORY

- ☑ Get a Wealth Journal
- ☐ Start Nightly Quality Questions
- ☐ Create your Income Statement
- ☐ Create your Balance Sheet
- ☐ Determine your current Net Worth
- ☐ Start a Money Diary to track your spending

....

- ☐ Create your Big Why
- ☐ Create your Financial Freedom Feast Vision
- ☐ Create your Financial Freedom Feast Menu
- ☐ Determine what type of Money Cook you were in the past
- ☐ Know Your Status—get your free credit reports
- ☐ Create your Easy Wealth Pie and Wealth Pots
- ☐ Develop a Spending Plan to achieve your spending targets
- ☐ Review past spending and Squeeze the Juice—find at least 5 percent
  to cut out
- ☐ Do the 1-Week Wealth Detox challenge—only spend on Security Soup items
  for a week
- ☐ Track your emotional spending triggers in your Wealth Journal

....

- ☐ Make the Expand Your Dough Recipe—Start an Automatic
  Investment plan

....

- ☐ Freeze one low-or no-fee credit card in a can of water :)
- ☐ Destroy your Debt—create and implement your Debt Destruction Plan

....

- ☐ Make a Will
- ☐ Make a Living Will
- ☐ Make an Enduring Power of Attorney
- ☐ Determine if you need term life insurance, the amount you need, and
  put it in place
- ☐ Review your home building and contents insurance (if applicable)

Cont. >

☐ Review your vehicle insurance (if applicable)

☐ Review your needs for disability and Income protection insurance

☐ Review your needs for medical and critical illness insurance

☐ Do a critical review of any other insurances you may have and determine if you really need them

. . . .

☐ Vacuuming–Do a physical clear-out of stuff that isn't adding value to your life from a minimum of one room

☐ Create an incompletions list. Against each incompletion, either complete it, schedule its completion, or declare it complete

☐ Determine your Time to Freedom–Complete your Freedom Feast Cooking Timer spreadsheet

☐ Personal Mastery–Decide which seminars, courses, teachers, and mentors you need to achieve your Financial Freedom

Appendix 2
The Wealth Chef Calendar

- Monthly -
Money Date Night Activities

SPENDING PLAN RECONCILIATION

- Download all transactions from online bank accounts.

- Review your Money Diary: add cash transactions to the list.

- Allocate your spending to a specific Wealth Pot category.

- Update your Income Statement.

- Check whether you are within your spending plan target percentage.

- If you are over in certain categories, look at the spending in detail and decide where you can make changes to get on target.

- Check if you made a profit this month!

DEBT DESTRUCTION

- Update your Debt Destruction Plan with new outstanding balances.

- If a debt has been paid off in the previous month, ensure the Debt Destroyer Fuel (DDF) and the old debt payment amount are rolled over to the new priority debt.

- Decide if you can increase your DDF—if so, add it to the priority debt payment.

- Look at your Debt Destruction date and celebrate, feeling great that your debt is being destroyed!

- Review any 0 percent credit cards. If the 0 percent interest rate period is due to expire in the next two months, find a new 0 percent deal and transfer the outstanding balance.

UPDATE YOUR WEALTH FILES

- File what you need to file.

- Update any tax information required for you or your business.

UPDATE YOUR WEALTH JOURNAL

- Review your juicy Financial Freedom Vision and your Big Why and update with anything new that you'd like to add.

- Review your quality questions.

- Are you still practicing your daily question ritual?

- Are you getting excited about your Wealth Feast every morning?

- Choose a new Wealth Book to read this month.

- Quarterly -

Complete your usual Money Date activities and add:

UPDATE YOUR NET WORTH

- Get updated statements from all your investment accounts.

- Get updated statements for all your Liabilities.

- Get updated valuation estimates for other Assets, such as property and business.

- Update your Balance Sheet.

- Plot your new Net Worth on your Freedom Feast Menu Planner.

- If you have achieved one of your Freedom Courses, have a huge celebration!

- Six Monthly -

Complete your Monthly and Quarterly activities and add:

INCOMPLETIONS REVIEW

- Create a fresh incompletions list.

- Against each incompletion, either complete it, schedule its completion, or declare it complete.

VACUUMING REVIEW

- Do a big physical clear-out of stuff gathering in your home and work spaces.

- Do a big emotional clear-out of stuff gathering in you that you need to let go of.

- Annually -

Make it a BIG MONEY DATE DAY

Complete your usual monthly, quarterly and six-monthly activities and add:

REFRESH YOUR WEALTH FEAST VISION AND YOUR BIG WHY

- Create a new vision board and get really excited about the life you've created and are creating.

CREDIT SCORE REVIEW

- Order your new free credit reports.

AUTOMATIC INVESTMENT PLAN REVIEW

- Review your AIP's annual performance.

- Decide if you want to change the tracker you're investing in or add another to your portfolio.

- Increase your AIP amount.

REVIEW ALL YOUR ASSETS

- Unemotionally review your Assets and make sure they're working hard for you.

- Determine the annual interest rate/return you're receiving from each Asset and for your portfolio as a whole.

- Decide if you need to change or remove any Assets.

- Determine where you may have gaps in your Asset mix.

- Recalculate your Time to Freedom, based on your average investment rate of return.

WEALTH DOCUMENTS REVIEW

- Review your Will.
- Update anything that has changed, especially in the event of divorce or death of a spouse or beneficiary.
- Ensure your executor is still appropriate.
- Update your Enduring Power of Attorney.
- Update your Living Will.
- Update any estate planning structures you may have, such as a Living Trust.

INSURANCE REVIEWS

- Do you need to increase or decrease your Life Insurance amounts? If so, review your Life Insurance savings tips in order to negotiate a good deal.
- Update the value of your home contents inventory.
- Get new quotes on your household, building, and vehicles' insurances. Review your insurance savings tips in order to negotiate a good deal.

PERSONAL MASTERY REVIEW

- Review your wealth plans for the year and commit to a Net Worth Target for the year.
- Decide which seminars, courses, teachers, and mentors you need in order to achieve your target.

Acknowledgments

Where do you start, and stop, when there are so many people to thank? Some have played a big role in the creation of this book, others a cameo—small, but vital to its success. No matter the scale, each one has been significant and I am infinitely grateful to everyone who has held me, encouraged me, bribed me, scolded me, listened to me, fed me, pushed me, and—most important—believed in me and what I have to share:

My infinitely patient hubby, Dave, who is my rock; my siblings and their families, Andrew and Kathleen, Penny and Nevil, Sue and Greg, and Cathy and Ray, who've always been there and always will; my soul sisters Debbie Beneke and Katharine Dever, who really see me and inspire me to explore all this life holds; my editors, Claire Elizabeth Terry and Oleguer Sarsanedas, who got this baby out of my hands and into the world; the incredibly talented Sara Bárcena for her fabulous illustrations, and finally, last but by no means least, all my clients who've trusted me with one of the most emotionally charged and personal subjects ever: their wealth journeys.

Thank you, also, to all the inspiring people I've had the privilege to work beside throughout my career and who, through their trust, support, and belief, have enabled me to become who I am today. The list is too long to include here, but you know who you are.

Huge appreciation and thanks to all the amazing teachers, mentors, and authors who've shared their gifts with me and given me the privilege of passing mine on: Tony Robbins, John Burley, Robert Kiyosaki, Pa Joof, Wayne Dyer, Topher Morrison, Warren Buffet, Benjamin Graham, Suze Orman, T. Harv Eker, Eckhart Tolle, Wayne Dyer, Jack Canfield, Marianne Williamson, and so many more.

Last but not least my cats Ruston and Bracken and my slobbery Spinone, Cara Mia. Thank you for walking on the keyboard, sitting on my lap and at my feet, making me go for walks to clear my head, and giving the most unconditional love and support ever!

About the Author

Ann is basically an adventurous
rolling stone, who loves to experience
different places by living in them.

She currently lives in Paris
with her hubby, two noisy cats, and
a slobbery Spinone (that's a dog);
but by the time you read this,
she could be anywhere!

You can find all the tools and resources referred
to throughout this book at The Wealth Chef website:
www.thewealthchef.com/thewealthchefbook
(CODE: RECIPES)

Printed in the United States
by Baker & Taylor Publisher Services